Cooking at My House

Cooking at My House
John Bishop

Douglas & McIntyre
Vancouver/Toronto

Douglas & McIntyre
2323 Quebec Street, Suite 201
Vancouver, British Columbia
V5T 4S7

Canadian Cataloguing in Publication Data
Bishop, John, 1944-
   Cooking at my house

   Includes index.
   ISBN 1-55054-727-5

   1. Cookery. I. Title.
TX714.B57 1999   641.5   C99-910691-0

Editing by Elizabeth Wilson
Design by George Vaitkunas
Colour photographs by John Sherlock
Black-and-white photographs by John Sherlock,
   Alastair Bird, George Vaitkunas and from the
   John Bishop archive
Printed and bound in Canada by Friesens
Printed on acid-free paper

The publisher gratefully acknowledges the assistance
of the Canada Council of the Arts and of the British
Columbia Ministry of Tourism, Small Business and
Culture. The publisher also acknowledges the finan-
cial support of the Government of Canada through
the Book Publishing Industry Development Program.
Canadä

John Bishop would like to thank Stephen Wong of
Mōt'iv and Ming Wo Ltd. and Ford's Flowers for din-
nerware and flowers used in the colour photographs,
and would like to acknowledge the ceramic artists
whose work appears here: Wayne Ngan, facing pages
33 and 96, and on page 71, Debbie Dewar, front cover
and page 130, and Huel Pottery, front cover.

Contents

Cranberry Sauce

1 qt cranberries 2 cook
2 cups water 3 minutes
Then add
1 teasp Ginger
Juice of 1 orange
Juice of 1 lemon
2 cups Brown sugar.
If too thin thicken with flour

To Serve Caviar

Mix caviar with chopped
separated raw
s + whites.
paringly on
toast These.
canapes or ap
te wonderful
t used to the st
flavour. They
d as appetizers
large dinners.
Caviar will keep in
as long as not exp
higher than 40° or 5

Introduction

❧

Cooking at home for me is truly recreational. Just give me my favourite music and a glass of wine, surround me with my favourite utensils and my Japanese knife, my old chopping board, my well-seasoned cast iron frying pan and I'm off to the races. Of course, some days it's just something you have to do, and as much as I enjoy it there's not a lot of time to spend.

Cooking my way through this book I realized again that coming up with meal plans and different recipes on a daily basis is extremely challenging. That said, most days I try to prepare complete meals, or the makings of, for Theresa and the kids before I head off to the restaurant.

The kickoff is getting wonderful ingredients. In the afternoon I go shopping, usually with no particular recipe in mind. Then I discover some organic greens, a free-range chicken, the first of the season's halibut or some local berries or fruit. We also get a box of organic vegetables delivered every week, and we never know exactly what will be in it.

Dishes evolve as I ask myself, what am I going to do with this? Many of the results are here in this book. The restaurant is also a great source of ideas, or sometimes I will develop recipe ideas at home for the chefs at work to try.

Some of the recipes in the book have been family favourites of my mother and sister. Pot pies, bread sauce, trifle and Welsh cakes are traditional British home cooking that I still love. Other recipes have been handed down by Theresa's Mom's family. And Theresa has contributed her share as well. She makes great vegetarian fare—I don't do *all* the cooking at our house.

I didn't grow up with fancy dishes. My dad was an avid gardener and we had chickens, so from the start I learned the value of freshness and simplicity. Later, when I worked in little country hotels, fresh and simple was the way you did it. Take your fish—just baptize it in melted butter and bake it.

Now, on days when I don't have much time, I'll apply those same principles: load a steamer up with washed greens or bok choi and on top of that a delicious piece of fresh halibut or seasoned lightly with salt and pepper, drizzled with a touch of sesame oil and chopped ginger, then steamed for ten minutes or so until just done.

Not that I always get to partake of it. Most nights I come home whacked out from the restaurant at around one in the morning. The house is dead quiet. Everyone else is in bed. I end up standing alone in the kitchen silently eating the cold leftovers. Remains of the day.

So that one night that I may be home is such a luxury. If we have time I really enjoy rattling those pots and pans. I've taken to rediscovering the beginnings of my apprenticeship: turning vegetables a little bit and cutting them finer and enjoying the process of cooking—making and refining stocks and sauces, grinding spices, baking, grilling, stirring—all this is what I love to do. It's what first attracted me to the kitchen. Some of the more involved or time-consuming recipes here came from those sessions.

Even at home, service time is special. When I start to develop a dish I also start thinking about how to serve it. I'll imagine a jewel-green salad in our big black stoneware bowls, or a chicken dish in a favourite terracotta casserole.

At the table I nearly always like to place large bowls and platters with the food and have people pass and take as much as they like (being careful not to knock over glasses in the process). That way, each dish is seen at its best. This is known as family-style dining, but I do it for dinner guests as well.

I love the creativity of setting the table, the ritual involved with napkins, bowls, candles, serving pieces on the table, placecards and menu cards, flower arrangements—lights, camera, action. Those little touches don't take long, but they make eating together an event and add a veneer of civilization. I think it's important for kids to know that they're part of something, and the cooking and food isn't just for their benefit.

But I do like to do special things for them. I've found that if you make it look like a french fry, they'll eat it. Anything pick-upable is kid food. Its fun to see them working at an artichoke, stripping away the leaves until they get to the heart. And they love it too.

Whether it's for my family or the restaurant, I want it to be right. I want to see people's faces and their reactions. Steam rising off a big bowl of corn on the cob or steamed clams, people reaching, smiling, anticipating, sopping up a sauce, enjoying—that's what it's all about for me.

Acknowledgments

Writing my second cookbook has been so exciting and rewarding. The time spent shopping, preparing and testing these recipes has brought me even closer to food and the importance of cooking at home. It has also rekindled lots of childhood memories of helping Mum get dinner ready after school instead of doing my homework. It has reminded me just how much I still love the art of it all—the circle as I call it. The farmer produces wonderful things, and you simply cook it and serve it to the people you love. Voilà.

My warmest appreciation first of all to the mums, Louise and Irene, my wife, Theresa, for her recipe contributions, editing and computer skills, and our children David and Gemma. I would like to thank my sister, Cherry, for her recipes and my brother, Adrian, for all the love he showers on our whole family.

I'm grateful to my assistant Carolyn Wallace for her invaluable help in testing the recipes. Thank you to Chef Dennis Green and manager Abel Jacinto and all the staff at Bishop's.

A special thanks to editor Elizabeth Wilson, photographer John Sherlock and designer extraordinaire George Vaitkunas.

And to Bruce and Jane, our Hornby Island hosts, in whose getaway home I love to cook up a storm.

Also, a tribute to the memory of our friend Bruce Fairbairn; not only was he a great musician, but also a wonderful host.

Finally, thanks to all home cooks who help nourish us.

Grilled Asparagus with Sundried Tomato Vinaigrette / 12

Beet Chips with Avocado Salad / 13

Crab or Vegetable Spring Rolls / 14

Salmon Terrine / 16

Smoked Salmon and Cream Cheese Pizzas / 18

Brie, Pear and Onion Strudel / 19

Stuffed Vine Leaves with Chardonnay Sauce / 20

Starters

Grilled Asparagus
with Sundried Tomato Vinaigrette

⚜

1 lb.	asparagus	500 g
1 Tbsp.	olive oil	15 mL
	salt and pepper	
	SUNDRIED TOMATO VINAIGRETTE	
1 Tbsp.	olive oil	15 mL
2 Tbsp.	minced red onion or shallot	30 mL
¼ cup	red wine or fruit vinegar	50 mL
½ cup	olive oil	125 mL
3 Tbsp.	finely chopped oil-packed sundried tomatoes	45 mL
	salt and pepper	
1 Tbsp.	chopped chives	15 mL

SERVES 4 AS APPETIZER

This dressing can also accompany green and yellow beans or leeks, and it makes a great dip for cooked artichokes.

The dish works fine if the vegetables are boiled or steamed, but grilling brings out a lovely sweetness.

Preheat barbecue or grill.

Wash and trim off the lower part of the asparagus. Peel the lower halves of the stalks if they are large and woody. Toss asparagus in a bowl with olive oil and salt and pepper.

Place asparagus on barbecue, being careful to position the stalks across the grill so they don't fall through. Grill for 5 to 10 minutes, turning once, until they're tender when pierced with the point of a knife.

SUNDRIED TOMATO VINAIGRETTE: Heat the 1 Tbsp. (15 mL) olive oil in a small frying pan and sauté the red onion until transparent. In a bowl mix all the other ingredients together. Add the sautéed onion. Season to taste.

To serve, place asparagus spears in a bundle on a salad plate. Drizzle with the vinaigrette. Garnish with purple chive flowers or fresh basil leaves.

Beet Chips
with Avocado Salad

❧

Everybody loves chips. These are so sweet and earthy tasting. They make a great hors d'oeuvre, and the chips can be made a day ahead and stored uncovered in a warm, dry place.

At the restaurant Chef Denis Green serves beet chips on top of mashed potatoes, which accompany a roast duck breast.

Try to buy the largest beets possible because they shrink in the drying process. In order to get the beets sliced thinly enough for this recipe use a vegetable slicer or mandoline. If the slices are too thick they won't dry properly.

BEET CHIPS: In medium saucepan on high heat, bring sugar and water to a boil. Remove from heat and let cool.

Meanwhile, slice beets very thinly (1/16 inch/1.5 mm thick, as for potato chips). Soak beet slices in cooled syrup for 1 hour. Preheat oven to 200°F (95°C).

Remove beets from syrup and arrange on a baking sheet lined with parchment paper. Bake for 1 hour. Turn over and bake for an additional half-hour, or until dry and crisp.

AVOCADO SALAD: Combine all the ingredients in a medium bowl and let sit for 1 hour before serving. Season to taste with salt and pepper.

BEET CHIPS		
2	large beets	2
1½ cups	water	375 mL
¾ cup	sugar	175 mL

AVOCADO SALAD		
2	ripe avocados, diced	2
2	shallots, minced	2
2 Tbsp.	chopped fresh cilantro	30 mL
2 Tbsp.	lime juice	30 mL
1 Tbsp.	olive oil	15 mL
	salt and pepper	

YIELDS ABOUT 40 CHIPS

Crab or Vegetable Spring Rolls

❦

People can't resist these delicious appetizers. They are the first to go at a party. They can be made in advance and then quickly reheated in the oven.

If you make both fillings, double the number of wrappers.

CRAB FILLING: Heat sesame oil and sauté carrot and ginger until softened. Combine with crab, lime juice and zest, and adjust seasoning.

VEGETABLE FILLING: Heat a large frying pan or soup pot on medium-high heat. Add sesame oil and stir-fry all of the vegetables and seasonings for approximately 10 minutes until they are softened and cooked. Remove from heat and allow to cool.

Lay out spring roll wrapper on a board or table. Mix up flour and water to form a paste. This will be used to seal the rolls before frying.

Place 2 to 3 Tbsp. (30 mL) of the filling on each wrapper and tightly roll up, tucking the ends as you roll. (Two Tbsp. per wrapper will give you about 20 spring rolls.) Brush the flap with a dab of paste, and press to seal.

CRAB FILLING		
1 Tbsp.	sesame oil	15 mL
1	large carrot, grated	1
1 tsp.	grated fresh ginger	5 mL
1 lb.	Dungeness crab meat	500 g
1	lime, juice and zest	1
	salt and pepper	

VEGETABLE FILLING		
2 Tbsp.	sesame oil	30 mL
3 cups	bean sprouts	750 mL
3 cups	shredded cabbage	750 mL
2 cups	peeled and coarsely grated carrots	500 mL
1 tsp.	grated ginger	5 mL
1	clove garlic, finely chopped	1
3	green onions, chopped	3
1 cup	sliced shiitake or other mushrooms	250 mL
	salt	

20	spring roll wrappers	20
2 Tbsp.	flour	30 mL
¼ cup	cold water	50 mL
	oil for frying	

YIELDS 20 SPRING ROLLS

Heat a medium frying pan on medium-high heat. Add vegetable oil to a depth of ½ inch (1.5 cm). When oil is hot but not smoking (350-375°F, 180-190°C), gently add 5 or 6 rolls and fry until golden brown on all sides. Place on paper towels and keep warm. Continue until all are cooked. Serve with Asian Dipping Sauce.

ASIAN DIPPING SAUCE: Blend all ingredients except cilantro in blender. Pour into serving bowl and stir in cilantro. Refrigerate until needed.

ASIAN DIPPING SAUCE		
3 Tbsp.	lime juice (juice of 2 limes)	50 mL
3 Tbsp.	rice vinegar	50 mL
3 Tbsp.	sesame oil	50 mL
1 Tbsp.	liquid honey	15 mL
1 Tbsp.	grated ginger	15 mL
2	cloves garlic, minced	2
¾ cup	hoisin sauce	175 mL
1 Tbsp.	chopped cilantro	

YIELDS 1½ CUPS (375 mL)

Salmon Terrine

ᓬ

2	eggs	2
1 lb.	salmon, centre cut	500 g
10-12	spears thin baby asparagus, thick bottom stalks removed	10-12
1	envelope gelatin	1
¼ cup	tepid water	50 mL
¼ cup	boiling water	50 mL
1¼ cups	warm water	300 mL
1 tsp.	lemon zest	5 mL
¼ tsp.	salt	1 mL

SERVES 6 TO 8
AS AN APPETIZER

Terrines are time consuming to put together, but the end result is marvellous, and nothing can go wrong. You really do feel like a professional chef when you have completed this dish. It's very impressive on a buffet, and the sauce works really well with all the other flavours.

Place eggs in cold water and bring to a boil. Boil eggs for 12 minutes, drain and plunge into cold water. Remove from shell, separate whites from yolks and finely chop each. Set aside.

Preheat oven to 375°(F (190°C).

Clean salmon, removing the skin and any bones. Cut the fillet into 6 strips, 6 inches long (15 cm). Place the strips of salmon on a parchment-lined baking sheet and roast for 5 to 10 minutes, until the salmon is opaque and cooked to medium doneness. Set aside. Turn oven off.

Blanch the asparagus in boiling water for 3 to 4 minutes, drain and plunge into cold water. Remove from water and set aside.

To prepare the aspic, place tepid water in a saucepan and sprinkle the gelatin powder over top. Pour boiling water into the mixture and stir constantly. Add warm water, lemon zest and salt to the gelatin, stirring until the powder is completely dissolved. Set aside.

To assemble the terrine, have the aspic, chopped egg, roasted salmon strips and asparagus on hand. You'll need a loaf pan that holds 4 cups (1 litre) and is approximately 3 x 7 inches (7.5 x 17.5 cm).

Pour ½ cup (125 mL) of the aspic into the loaf pan and sprinkle 2 Tbsp. (30 mL) of chopped egg white and 1 Tbsp. (15 mL) of chopped egg yolk over top. Place the terrine in the freezer for 5 minutes until set. Next, place a layer of 3 salmon strips in the mould, followed by a layer of blanched asparagus tips. Place another layer of 2 Tbsp. (30 mL) chopped egg white and 1 Tbsp. (15 mL) chopped egg yolk and then top this with the remaining 3 salmon strips. Fill the loaf pan with the rest of the gelatin mixture. If the gelatin has started to solidify, simply warm it over low heat until it melts.

Put a light pressure on the terrine with your hand to ensure that the gelatin has covered all the ingredients. Wrap with plastic and place in the refrigerator on a level rack to set overnight.

To unmould the terrine; fill a roasting pan about ¾ full with hot water. Dip the terrine mould into the water for 5 seconds. Invert onto a rectangular serving plate. Dip a sharp knife in hot water. Cut the terrine into 6 to 8 slices using a sawing motion. Serve with the sauce.

BASIL SAUCE: Place all of the ingredients in a blender or food processor and blend well together until the sauce turns green. Check for seasoning, chill and serve.

BASIL SAUCE

1 cup	mayonnaise	250 mL
1 cup	sour cream	250 mL
1 cup	basil leaves	250 mL
1 Tbsp.	lemon juice	15 mL
1 Tbsp.	Dijon mustard	15 mL
	salt to taste	
1 tsp.	creamed horseradish	5 mL

Smoked Salmon
and Cream Cheese Pizzas

❦

½ lb.	puff pastry	250 g
¼ cup	cream cheese	50 mL
¼ cup	sour cream	50 mL
1 sprig	dill, chopped	1 sprig
3 oz.	smoked salmon, thinly sliced	90 g
½	small onion, thinly sliced	½
1½ tsp.	vegetable oil	7 mL

YIELDS 6

These seafood pizzas are very quick to prepare. They can be served as an hors d'oeuvre or on a buffet hot or cold. Wrap them up in waxed paper and take them along on a picnic.

The smoked salmon can be substituted with prosciutto.

Roll out puff pastry on a floured board to a thickness of ⅛ inch (3 mm) and cut into 6-inch (15 cm) rounds or squares. Place on a baking sheet lined with parchment paper and prick with a fork. Refrigerate until needed.

Blend together cream cheese, sour cream and dill and spread on pastry sections. Top with smoked salmon and sliced onions. Brush lightly with vegetable oil and bake at 400°F (200°C) for 15 minutes, or until pastry is golden and cooked through.

Brie, Pear and Onion Strudel

❦

This is ideal for a buffets, special occasions or even for picnics, as it can be prepared in advance. I love the combination of the onion and the sweet pear flavours melded together by the creaminess of the Brie cheese.

Fry onion slices gently in oil on medium heat until they are brown and caramelized. Set aside to cool. Peel, core and thinly slice pear.

Roll out one block of pre-made or purchased puff pastry to a thickness of ⅛ inch (3 mm) in a 9 x 12-inch (23 x 30 cm) rectangle. Lay out thinly sliced Brie, then the pear slices and the cooked onions down the centre third of the pastry leaving a third clear on each side. Fold the left side of pastry over the filling to cover it. Using a pastry cutter or knife, cut horizontal lines ½ inch (1.5 cm) apart on the right-hand side of pastry. Brush the top of the folded-over pastry with half of the egg white. Fold the first and last strips of pastry across the seal. Fold the next strip on an angle and cross the next one over it to form an X pattern. Repeat along the top in a crisscross pattern. Brush the top of the pastry with the rest of the egg white mixture. Transfer to a baking sheet lined with parchment paper and let rest in the fridge for 10 minutes.

Preheat oven to 350°F (190°C).

Bake the strudel for 30 minutes, until the pastry is golden brown. Allow to cool for 10 minutes then cut into slices 1¼ to 2 inches (3 to 5 cm) thick and serve.

1	medium onion, sliced	1
1 Tbsp.	vegetable oil	15 mL
1	ripe pear (about 8 oz./250 g)	1
7 oz.	puff pastry	200 g
4½ oz.	round of Brie, chilled	125 g
1	egg white, slightly beaten	1

SERVES 4 TO 6
AS AN APPETIZER

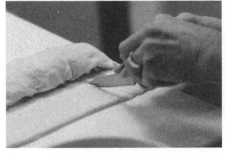

Stuffed Vine Leaves
with Chardonnay Sauce

½ lb.	prawn tails, peeled and deveined, coarsely chopped	250 g
½ lb.	lean pork, minced (ask the butcher to double mince this for you)	250 g
2 Tbsp.	chopped cilantro	30 mL
2	cloves garlic, finely minced	2
1 tsp.	grated fresh ginger	5 mL
1 tsp.	crushed coriander seeds	5 mL
1 Tbsp.	lemon juice	15 mL
	salt and pepper	
1 bottle	whole vine leaves or 12 fresh young vine leaves	1 bottle

SAUCE

1 Tbsp.	butter	15 mL
2 Tbsp.	chopped shallots	30 mL
2 cups	Chardonnay	500 mL
2 cups	whipping cream	500 mL
¼ cup	cold butter cut into chunks	50 mL
12	seedless grapes	12
	salt and white pepper	

SERVES 6

The use of vine leaves goes back to ancient times in Europe. Here we are incorporating seafood and pork together with the wonderful Asian influences of ginger and cilantro.

This is an excellent starter for a wine dinner. Try to serve the same wine that you use in the sauce. If you can, these are best made with fresh young vine leaves. Remove stems, wash and stuff.

Combine prawn, pork, cilantro, garlic, ginger and coriander in a large bowl. Season this mixture with the lemon juice and salt and pepper. Divide the mixture into 12 parts.

Flatten 12 vine leaves. If using bottled vine leaves you should rinse them first and pat dry. Place a portion of the prawn/pork mixture in the centre of each. Starting at one end, roll the vine leaf around the mixture, forming a tight roll and fold the ends under to form a neat package. Repeat with the remaining leaves.

Place the stuffed vine leaves in a steamer over boiling water and cover. Steam for 6 to 7 minutes, or until firm.

SAUCE: Place a saucepan over low heat and melt 1 Tbsp. (15 mL) butter. Add shallots and sauté until soft. Add the wine and reduce over high heat to 2 Tbsp. (30 mL). Add the cream and reduce over medium heat by half. Turn the heat to low. Whisk in the cold butter piece by piece, until it is all absorbed. Then add coarsely chopped grapes. Season with salt and white pepper.

To serve, spoon a ladle of sauce onto a preheated plate and arrange 2 stuffed leaves on top.

Soups

Gazpacho Andalucía

1½ lbs.	fresh tomatoes cut into quarters	750 mL
1	medium cucumber, peeled and cut into ¼-inch (5 mm) cubes	1
1	medium green pepper, seeded, cut in ¼-inch (5 mm) cubes	1
6	small cloves garlic, peeled and crushed	6
⅔ cup	olive oil	150 mL
1 Tbsp.	cumin seed, crushed	15 mL
3 cups	tomato juice	750 mL
4 Tbsp.	red wine vinegar	65 mL
	salt and pepper to taste	

GARNISH

2 cups	fresh bread croutons, not toasted	500 mL
1 cup	finely diced green pepper	250 mL
1 cup	finely diced onion	250 mL
1 cup	finely diced cucumber	250 mL
1 cup	fresh tomato, blanched, seeded and finely chopped	250 mL

SERVES 10 TO 12

This classic Spanish cold soup is almost a meal in itself, especially at lunch on a hot summer's day, accompanied by a glass of dry sherry. It is a great opportunity to use summer-ripened vegetables.

In a blender, combine all ingredients and blend to a cream soup consistency. Check seasoning and pour into a plastic or glass container. Chill until needed.

To serve, place the garnishes in small individual serving bowls. Place them all on a large round platter on the table, so that people can help themselves. Then serve up the chilled soup in chilled bowls.

Fresh Green Pea Soup with Mint

❦

This is one of my favourite soups. It is the essence of green peas, and so easy to prepare. It can also be served as an elegant and colourful sauce to accompany such things as poached salmon, halibut or scallops. The secret to keeping the colour so intense is to prepare it just before serving, and not overcook it.

Place peas, mint, salt and sugar in a soup pot. Cover with cold water. Bring to a boil on medium-high heat. Simmer for 3 to 5 minutes, until the peas are cooked. Remove from the burner and blend, either in a food mill or electric blender, until completely smooth. Pour soup back into pot and reheat before serving.

To serve, pour hot soup into warm soup bowls. The soup can be served plain like this or with chunks of goat cheese dotted around for extra flavour.

4½ cups	peas, fresh or frozen	1.1 L
6	fresh mint leaves	6
¾ tsp.	salt	4 mL
1 tsp.	sugar	5 mL
4 cups	cold water	1 L
4 oz.	goat cheese (optional)	125 g

SERVES 6

Garden Carrot Soup

2 Tbsp.	butter	30 mL
2	medium onions, chopped (1¼ cups/300 mL)	2
4½ cups	peeled, chopped carrots	1.1 L
1 Tbsp.	peeled, grated ginger	15 mL
7 cups	water or chicken stock	1.75 L
	zest of 1 orange	
⅓ cup	orange juice (1-2 oranges)	75 mL
	salt and pepper	

SERVES 6

We very often make this soup on our Hornby Island holidays, using Jim Gordon's organically grown carrots. I actually prefer to make it with water rather than stock because you get a purer taste.

In a large soup pot on medium heat, melt butter and sauté onions until soft. Add carrots and ginger and sauté another 2 to 3 minutes. Add cold water or stock. Simmer uncovered for 1 hour.

Transfer to blender or food processor and purée. Return to pot and add orange zest and juice. Season with salt and pepper to taste. Gently reheat and serve.

Roasted Eggplant and Garlic Soup

I didn't grow up eating eggplant, or even eating very much garlic, but as a grown-up I very quickly developed a taste for these wonderful Mediterranean vegetables. The roasting of the eggplant and garlic is very important to the flavour and intensity of this soup. And, of course, soup always tastes better the next day.

Cut whole head of garlic in half and rub oil all over it. Place garlic, cut sides down, and whole eggplant on a lightly oiled roasting pan. Roast for 30 minutes at 400°F (200°C) until eggplant is tender when pierced with a knife. Remove from oven and allow to cool.

In a large pot, melt butter and sauté chopped onions until soft. Roughly chop roasted eggplant (no need to peel) and squeeze garlic cloves from the skin. Add to onions. Add water or chicken stock. Simmer for 1 hour. Purée, then add the cream. Season with salt and pepper. Reheat and garnish with Garlic Croutons.

GARLIC CROUTONS: Heat a frying pan on medium heat; add the butter. When butter is melted add garlic slices and cook for 1 to 2 minutes. Add the bread cubes and fry on low heat until crispy and golden brown. Turn occasionally so bread is golden on all sides.

1	head garlic	1
	vegetable oil	
1 1-lb.	eggplant	1 500g
2 Tbsp.	butter	30 mL
1¼ cups	chopped onions	300 mL
6 cups	water or chicken stock	1.5 L
2 tsp.	salt	10 mL
½ tsp.	pepper	2 mL
½ cup	cream	125 mL

GARLIC CROUTONS

1 cup	white bread, cut into ½-inch cubes (1 cm)	250 mL
2	cloves garlic, peeled and sliced	2
2 Tbsp.	butter or olive oil	25 mL

SERVES 6

Chilled Blueberry Soup

✦

3 cups	blueberries, cleaned	750 mL
3 cups	water	750 mL
½ cup	white wine	125 mL
⅓ cup	sugar	75 mL
½ cup	orange juice	125 mL
1½ cups	carbonated mineral water or soda water	375 mL
2 Tbsp.	plain yogurt for garnish	25 mL

SERVES 6 TO 8

Soups made from summer berries make wonderfully refreshing starters to a patio lunch or picnic. They're easy to prepare and can be made ahead and chilled. I like to garnish them with sprigs of lemon balm or mint and a swirl of plain yogurt.

In a large pot combine blueberries, water, wine, sugar and orange juice. Bring to a boil and then reduce heat and simmer for 2 to 3 minutes. Remove the soup from the heat and let cool. Pass soup through a food mill or purée in a food processor. Refrigerate to chill. Just before serving, whisk in carbonated mineral water.

To make a yogurt swirl, whisk yogurt smooth with a fork, then simply place 1 tsp. (5 mL) of plain yogurt in the centre of each bowl. Using the point of a knife make a figure eight to distribute the yogurt in an artful way.

Spicy Salmon Chowder

You can make this with salmon, snapper, cod, halibut or any combination of favourite fish. I really enjoy spicy food, so for myself I would probably add more Tabasco sauce, or even a chopped green jalapeño chili.

Try to find a large soup tureen and soup ladle to serve this. It's so nice to be able to bring it out and place it in the center of the table and ladle out the piping-hot chowder.

Melt butter in a soup pot on medium-high heat. Sauté vegetables in butter until soft, approximately 10 minutes. Add wine, water and chopped tomatoes with their juice. Simmer uncovered for 35 to 40 minutes. Then add salmon cubes and Tabasco. Simmer covered without stirring for 15 minutes, then serve.

2 Tbsp.	butter	25 mL
2	onions, chopped	2
1	red pepper, seeded and chopped	1
2	ribs celery, chopped	2
1	medium head fennel, chopped	1
1	clove garlic, chopped	1
2	carrots, diced (1½ cups/375 mL)	2
1 cup	white wine	250 mL
2 cups	water	500 mL
28-oz.	tin stewed tomatoes, chopped	796 mL
½ lb.	fresh salmon fillet, cubed	250 g
1 tsp.	Tabasco	5 mL

SERVES 6

Potato and Watercress Soup

1 Tbsp.	butter	15 mL
1	medium white onion, chopped	1
1	stalk celery, chopped	1
1	baby leek, washed & chopped (including leaves)	1
2	cloves garlic, chopped	2
2	large potatoes, peeled and chopped	2
1	bunch watercress, leaves and stems, washed	1
10 cups	water	2.5 L
½ cup	whipping cream	125 mL
	salt and pepper	

SERVES 8

Potato and watercress make an all-seasons combination. The peppery quality of the watercress makes it a wonderful warm winter soup. But it also sparkles when served chilled in the summer.

Place a large soup pot over medium-high heat. Melt butter, then add chopped onion, celery, leek and garlic. Cover and cook for 5 minutes until the vegetables are transparent and partially cooked. Then add the chopped potatoes and watercress. Cover with cold water and bring to simmer. Cook uncovered for approximately 1 hour. Remove from the heat and process in a food mill or a blender until smooth. Add whipping cream and season with salt and pepper. Gently reheat and serve.

A garnish of lightly whipped cream can be added, with a scattering of watercress leaves.

Everyday Simple Soup

This is a recipe from my sister, Cherry. The variations are endless. Spring vegetables bring lightness. In summer, beets can add richness of colour along with the selection of green vegetables. Autumn brings the pumpkins and the harvest of roots ready to make the comforting soups for the colder winter days. Peas, beans and lentils or grains can be added for bulk.

Heat the oil in a soup pot and sauté the onion and garlic until tender. Add the vegetables and lentils. Add stock, tomato paste, herbs and bran. Bring to boil. Stir well and season with salt and pepper. Simmer covered on low heat for approximately 20 minutes. It can simmer longer if necessary. Stir in the juice of the orange about 10 minutes before the end, and adjust the seasoning. Sprinkle with fresh chopped parsley and serve with crusty bread and butter.

1 Tbsp.	olive oil	15 mL
1	large onion, chopped	1
2	cloves garlic, minced	2
2	carrots, sliced	2
2	new potatoes, diced	2
2	fresh tomatoes, chopped	2
¼ cup	orange lentils	50 mL
4 cups	chicken or vegetable stock, or water	1 L
1 Tbsp.	tomato paste	15 mL
2 Tbsp.	chopped parsley	30 mL
1 tsp.	chopped thyme	5 ml
1 tsp.	bran	5 mL
1½ tsp.	salt	7 mL
½ tsp.	white or black pepper	2 mL
	juice of 1 orange	

SERVES 4

Crab and Roasted Pepper Bisque

❦

2	red peppers	2
2	yellow peppers	2
⅓ cup	olive oil	75 mL
4 cups	Clamato juice	1 L
2 cups	peeled and chopped carrots (4 medium)	500 mL
2 cups	crab stock (page 153) or clam nectar	500 mL
	salt and pepper	

GARNISH

1 cup	curried whipped cream	250 mL
1 cup	fresh crabmeat	250 mL
1 Tbsp.	chopped cilantro	15 mL

CURRIED WHIPPED CREAM

1 cup	whipping cream, whipped	250mL
½ tsp.	mild curry powder	2 mL

SERVES 8

I first prepared this seafood soup on Hornby Island for a group of friends at Arnie Olson's farm. Artist Toni Onley enjoyed it so much that after he flew back home he phoned and asked me for the recipe, which of course I hadn't written down yet. Anyway, here it is.

I prepared the stock from fresh crab that we purchased at Fanny Bay on our way up to Hornby. But Toni tells me it's just as good made with clam nectar.

Preheat oven to 450°F (230°C).

Rub the red and yellow peppers with olive oil. Place in a pan and roast in oven for 10 to 15 minutes, turning the peppers every few minutes.

Place the peppers in a bowl and cover tightly with plastic wrap. Let cool for 30 minutes, as this will make it easier to remove the skin. Cut each pepper in half, peel off the skin and then remove the core and seeds.

In a large soup pot, place all of the ingredients except salt and pepper. Bring to a boil and simmer for approximately 30 to 40 minutes on medium heat. Remove soup from heat and allow to cool.

When cool, place in blender or food mill and process until smooth. Return to the burner on low heat.

Check seasoning and add salt and pepper to taste. Serve in hot bowls with 1 Tbsp. (15 mL) curried whipped cream floating on top. Garnish with fresh crabmeat and chopped cilantro.

CURRIED WHIPPED CREAM: Combine curry powder with the whipped cream. Cover and refrigerate for 20 minutes before serving to allow the flavour of the curry powder to infuse.

Salads

Watercress Salad

ﬂ

2	bunches watercress	2

	VINAIGRETTE	
2 Tbsp.	white wine vinegar	30 mL
	juice of ½ lemon	
6 Tbsp.	olive oil	90 mL
	freshly ground black pepper	
1 tsp.	capers	5 mL
1	small clove garlic, crushed	1
½ tsp.	Dijon mustard	2 mL
	toasted pine nuts for garnish	

SERVES 4 TO 6

The flavoursome dressing goes very well with peppery watercress. Some toasted pine nuts add an extra element.

This is a nice accompaniment to barbecued meat or fish.

Wash the watercress well with lots of cold water. Drain and pat dry. Trim all the thick stems from the bottom of the cress, leaving mostly leaves for the salad. Place in a salad bowl and lightly toss with the vinaigrette.

VINAIGRETTE: Place the vinegar and lemon juice in a small bowl. Add the olive oil and whisk in all of the remaining ingredients.

FACING PAGE
Brie, Pear and Onion Strudel, page 19;
Watercress Salad

Romaine, Red Apple and Olive Salad

Romaine is very special in the salad family—it is one of the nicest and crunchiest of lettuces.

This recipe combines sweet red apples with tangy apple cider vinegar and salty olives.

VINAIGRETTE: To prepare the dressing, whisk the oil and vinegar together and season with salt and pepper.

Wash and dry romaine and break leaves into bite-sized pieces. Place romaine in salad bowl. Quarter, core and thinly slice apple and add to romaine along with whole stuffed green olives. Pour the dressing over the salad. Toss together and serve on chilled plates.

	VINAIGRETTE	
3 Tbsp.	olive oil	45 mL
1 Tbsp.	cider vinegar or white wine vinegar	15 mL
	pinch salt	
	pinch pepper	
1	head romaine lettuce	1
1	medium red apple	1
⅓ cup	pimento-stuffed green olives	75 mL

SERVES 4

FACING PAGE
Black Thai Rice with Prawns and Ginger, page 86;
Asian Stir Fry, page 58

Fresh Corn and Orzo Salad

1 cup	orzo, uncooked	250 mL
3	apples or pears, peeled and finely chopped	3
2	cobs corn (or 1 cup/250 mL kernels)	2
3 Tbsp.	chopped fresh basil	45 mL
½ cup	olive oil	125 mL
2 Tbsp.	lemon juice	30 mL
½ tsp.	salt	2 mL

SERVES 8

This dish is great for a summer buffet or a potluck. It is very fresh tasting and goes really well with barbecued salmon or grilled chicken.

Cook orzo in a large pot of boiling salted water for 8 to 10 minutes, until tender. Drain and run under cold water. Set aside.

Bring a pot of water to a boil. Add corn and return to boil. Remove from heat, cover and let corn sit in water for 5 minutes. Drain and run under cold water. With a sharp knife, remove corn from cobs and set aside.

In a large bowl, combine cooked orzo, chopped apples or pears, blanched corn, chopped basil, olive oil, lemon juice and salt. Mix all ingredients together and let stand in the refrigerator for 2 hours before serving.

New Potato Salad
with Buttermilk Dressing

This fresh-tasting potato salad is great served with chicken or salmon, or just with mixed greens. It can easily be taken along on a picnic—but keep it cool.

Scrub potatoes well. Using a vegetable peeler, remove a half-inch (1.5 cm) band of skin from the centre of each potato.

Start potatoes in cold salted water and boil for approximately 15 to 20 minutes until potatoes are cooked and tender when pricked with a sharp knife. Drain and place in a salad bowl.

In small bowl, mix the mayonnaise, buttermilk, parsley and mint leaves. Toss dressing through the potatoes. Taste for seasoning.

These potatoes can be served either hot or cold. If you plan to serve the next day, cover with plastic wrap and refrigerate. They will keep well this way for 3 to 4 days. It's a good idea to toss the potatoes again just before serving to make sure they're properly dressed.

VARIATION: Replace the potatoes with an equal quantity of peeled and chopped cucumber. This makes a refreshing salad and an excellent accompaniment to spicy foods like curries.

¾ lb.	small new potatoes (about 14)	350 g
3 Tbsp.	mayonnaise	45 mL
3 Tbsp.	buttermilk	45 mL
1 Tbsp.	chopped parsley	15 mL
2 Tbsp.	chopped fresh mint	30 mL
1 tsp.	salt	5 mL

SERVES 4

Shrimp and Pear Salad

❧

1 lb.	peeled shrimp	500g
1	whole ripe pear, peeled and cut into small chunks	1
1 cup	cooked corn kernels	250 mL
1 Tbsp.	chopped fresh basil leaves	15 mL
2 Tbsp.	chopped cilantro	25 mL
1 Tbsp.	lemon juice	15 mL
3 Tbsp.	olive oil	45 mL
	salt and pepper	

SERVES 6

This is a summer seaside-holiday recipe. Try to find the very largest of hand-peeled shrimp. Also make sure that the pears are properly ripened, as the overall taste of this dish relies on the marriage of sweet fresh shrimp and sweet ripe pear flavours.

Place shrimp, chunks of pear and cooked corn kernels in a bowl and add chopped basil and cilantro. Dress with the lemon juice and olive oil, season with salt and pepper. Toss together and refrigerate for 30 minutes to an hour before serving to allow the flavours to come out more.

This salad can be served in a leaf cup such as radicchio or butter lettuce. Garnish with basil or cilantro leaves. For people who might like things spicy, a small jalapeño pepper can be finely diced and added to give extra zing.

Red Lettuce, Pink Grapefruit, Avocado and Crabmeat Salad

This colourful salad is also great with shrimp or lobster or it can be served as a vegetarian salad without the seafood.

For the crispest greens, wash and dry them at least an hour before dinner and put them in the fridge in a plastic bag.

VINAIGRETTE: Pour the vinegar, mustard, olive oil and honey into a salad bowl. Season with salt and pepper and whisk together.

Wash and dry lettuce and tear into bite-sized pieces. Peel grapefruit and cut into segments, making sure to remove all of the pith and peel. Peel avocado and cut into eighths.

Add the red leaf lettuce, grapefruit and avocado to dressing in bowl. Toss carefully together so as not to mash the fruit.

Divide the tossed salad onto 4 plates, then top with the fresh crab and serve.

VINAIGRETTE		
1 Tbsp.	red wine vinegar	15 mL
1 tsp.	Dijon mustard	5 mL
3 Tbsp.	olive oil	45 mL
1 tsp.	liquid honey	5 mL
	salt and pepper	
1	head red leaf lettuce	1
1	large pink grapefruit	1
1	ripe avocado	1
½ lb.	fresh crabmeat, preferably claw meat	250 g

SERVES 4

Barbecued Salmon, Eggplant and Mango Salad

❦

	VINAIGRETTE	
2 Tbsp.	olive oil	30 mL
1 Tbsp.	balsamic vinegar	15 mL
	salt and pepper	
2 3-4 oz.	salmon fillets	250 g
	salt and pepper	
2	small Japanese eggplants	2
	olive oil	
1	mango, ¼-inch dice (5 mm)	1
4	small tomatoes, quartered	4
2 Tbsp.	finely diced red onion	30 mL
2 Tbsp.	diced celery	30 mL
1 Tbsp.	chopped basil	15 mL
	salt and pepper	
6	large green pitted olives	6

SERVES 2

I was in that situation one day of having to use what was at hand. These were the ingredients I had to work with, and though I would never have thought up this combination, it turned out to be delicious. The grilled flavours combine well with the sweetness of the mango. And it's ideal for using up leftover barbecued salmon.

VINAIGRETTE: Combine olive oil and balsamic vinegar. Add salt and pepper to taste.

Season salmon fillets with salt and pepper. Grill for 3½ to 5 minutes per side until just done. Set aside. When cool flake with a fork.

Cut eggplants in half lengthwise. Brush with olive oil. Grill for approximately 8 to 10 minutes each side on medium-high heat.

Meanwhile combine flaked salmon, mango, tomatoes, onion, celery and basil. Add salt and pepper to taste. Toss gently with vinaigrette.

Place salad on cold dinner plates. Garnish with warm grilled eggplant halves and scatter with olives.

Starches

Steamed Basmati Rice

1 cup	basmati rice	250 mL
2 tsp.	butter or vegetable oil	10 mL
1	cinnamon stick	1
4	cloves	4
1½ cups	cold water	375 mL
½ tsp.	salt	2 mL

SERVES 4 TO 6

We love to eat all kinds of rice, but aromatic basmati is our favourite. It can be served as an accompaniment to many kinds of dishes, and is particularly great with the Lentil Hot Pot (page 65).

Place rice in a sieve and rinse under running water until the water runs clear. Set aside and allow to drain.

Place butter or oil in a heavy medium-sized saucepan. Add cinnamon stick and cloves and fry for a few seconds. Put rice in pot and stir until rice is coated with oil. Pour cold water into pot with salt. Bring to boil over high heat.

Put a tight-fitting lid on pot and turn down to very low. Cook for 18 to 20 minutes. Remove from heat and let stand another 5 minutes, without taking the lid off. This allows the rice to absorb any remaining steam. Fluff rice with a fork and serve.

VARIATION: When making basmati rice to be served with a curry, you can use ⅓ tin coconut milk to replace an equal amount of water.

Butternut Squash Risotto

This is a recipe that we make at home quite often because it is so easy to prepare. We vary the type of squash depending on the availability. At the restaurant we serve it the whole year round. It's great made with pumpkin and served with roast chicken or grilled scallops.

Melt butter over medium heat and gently sauté onions and garlic with thyme until almost transparent. Add squash and rice and sauté until grains are slightly transparent.

Season with salt and pepper and deglaze pan with wine. Add enough stock to cover rice by ½ inch (1.5 cm) and simmer uncovered, adding stock when needed so rice remains just covered with liquid. Stir occasionally.

When rice is 90 percent cooked (about 30 minutes) add cream, spinach and cheese and finish cooking until still creamy but thick enough to mound slightly on the plate.

2 Tbsp.	butter	30 mL
1 cup	diced onion	250 mL
1 tsp.	minced garlic	5 mL
1 Tbsp.	chopped fresh thyme	15 mL
2 cups	butternut squash in ½-inch (2.5 cm) dice	500 mL
2 cups	arborio rice	500 mL
	salt and pepper	
½ cup	white wine	125 mL
4 cups	chicken or vegetable stock	1 L
1 cup	cream	250 mL
1 cup	fresh spinach leaves	250 ml
¼ cup	grated Parmesan cheese	50 mL

SERVES 6 TO 8

Cranberry Couscous

🌿

2 Tbsp.	butter	25 mL
½ cup	chopped onion	125 mL
1	clove garlic, minced	1
½ cup	dried cranberries	125 mL
1 tsp.	lemon zest	5 mL
12 oz.	couscous	375 g
1 tsp.	salt	5 mL
2 cups	chicken stock or water, boiling	500 mL
1 Tbsp.	chopped parsley	15 mL

SERVES 6

This dish makes a nice accompaniment to roast chicken or any poultry recipe. I've added the cranberries to give it a seasonal taste.

Melt the butter in a frying pan over medium heat. Sauté onion and garlic until transparent, being careful not to burn the garlic. Add cranberries, lemon zest, couscous, salt and boiling liquid. Mix together. Pour mixture into a 6 cup (1.5 L) Pyrex baking dish. Cover the dish with foil and bake at 375°F (190°C) for 15 minutes. Remove from oven, add fresh parsley and fluff with a fork. Serve hot or cold.

Oven Fries

🌿

4	large baking potatoes, peeled	4
4 tsp.	vegetable oil	20 mL
¼ tsp.	celery salt	1 mL
¼ tsp.	salt	1 mL

YIELDS 24 FRIES

I often make these lower-fat fries as an after-school snack, and when the kids have friends over. They are quicker and healthier than deep frying. When I make these for the kids, I like to make paper cones to serve them in. The kids get a kick out of that. They think they are getting fast food—minus the toys.

Preheat oven to 400°F (200°C) and place roasting pan inside to heat up. Cut potatoes lengthwise into double-sized French fries: approximately six per potato. Heat a nonstick frying pan on medium-high heat. Toss the potatoes with the vegetable oil and seasonings. Place them in the pan and fry to lightly brown them.

Pour them onto preheated roasting pan and roast for approximately 15 minutes, until cooked and browned, turning occasionally.

Potato Dumplings
with Basil

The sesame oil and basil combination gives these little dumplings an oriental twist. The secret to making them irresistible is to serve them right out of the pan, golden brown and sizzling.

Choose baking potatoes for this recipe, because they're drier and starchier.

Start potatoes in cold salted water and boil until cooked. Drain completely dry, then mash or put potatoes through a potato ricer to remove any lumps. Put the mashed potatoes into a mixing bowl and add the chopped basil and seasoning. Mix in the flour to form a ball.

Next, divide the mixture into four sections. One by one roll out each piece on a well-floured board to form a long sausage shape approximately ¾ inch (2 cm) in diameter. Cut each roll into 1-inch (2.5 cm) lengths.

Fill a large pot ¾ full of salted water and bring to a simmer over medium-high heat. Slowly begin to poach the dumplings 1 roll at a time. The dumplings will float to the surface when they are cooked. Remove from the pot, drain, and place them in a cold water bath for 2 minutes to cool. Remove from the cold water bath and lay on a tray covered with waxed paper.

Heat the sesame oil in a large nonstick frying pan on medium-high heat. Add the dumplings and quickly fry until golden brown on all sides, then serve.

1 lb.	baking potatoes, peeled and chopped	500 g
1 Tbsp.	chopped basil leaves	15 mL
	salt and pepper	
1 cup	flour	250 mL
2 Tbsp.	sesame oil	30 mL

SERVES 4

Black Olive and Crunchy Garlic Mashed Potatoes

❦

2 lbs.	russet potatoes, peeled	1 kg
2 Tbsp.	vegetable oil	30 mL
4	cloves garlic, sliced	4
4 Tbsp.	heavy cream	60 mL
2 Tbsp.	olive oil	30 mL
½ cup	black olives, chopped	125 mL
	salt and pepper to taste	

SERVES 4

This is the Rocky Road of the mashed potato world. Crunchy garlic, black olives and good olive oil make a great trio.

Start potatoes in cold salted water and boil until cooked. Drain well and mash or put through ricer.

Heat vegetable oil in small pan over medium-low heat. Gently fry garlic slices until golden brown and crispy. Remove from heat immediately. Too-quick cooking or overcooking will burn the garlic and make it bitter.

Drain off the oil and add the garlic to the potatoes along with the cream, olive oil and chopped olives. Stir well. Season with salt and pepper. Keep warm until needed.

Potato Cheese Puffs

❦

3	russet potatoes, peeled and quartered (2 cups/500 mL mashed)	3
1 Tbsp.	butter	15 mL
	salt and pepper	
½ cup	grated cheddar cheese	125 mL
1¼ cups	cornflakes, slightly crushed	300 mL

YIELDS 8

These make a good kids' party dish as an alternative to fries. They're also a good way to use up any leftover mashed potatoes. For grown-ups, try them with a teaspoon (5 mL) of minced onion and 2 tsp. (10 mL) fresh marjoram added. I usually leave that out when making them for the children. They are great hot or cold.

Preheat oven to 400°F (200°C).

Boil potatoes until tender. Drain, mash with butter and season with salt and pepper. Add cheese and mix together well. Allow to cool. Shape into balls and roll in cornflakes. Flatten into cakes and bake on oiled baking sheet for 20 minutes.

Scallion Griddle Cakes

Cooking like this always reminds me of growing up in Wales, or later, living in Ireland. There, they always refer to this type of dish as a fry-up, the best known one being Bubble and Squeak, a potato-and-cabbage combination. Even today in some remote parts of those countries griddle cakes are still made over an open fire on a heavy griddle iron. At home we have a favourite cast-iron griddle that we use on the stove top.

4	medium baking potatoes (about 1 lb./500 g)	4
⅓ cup	chopped green onions	75 mL
1	egg yolk	1
½ tsp.	salt	2 mL
	pinch pepper	
2 Tbsp.	vegetable oil or butter	30 mL

YIELDS 4 CAKES

Bake potatoes with skins on for 1 hour at 400°F (200°C). Remove from the oven and allow to cool for 5 minutes.

Peel the potatoes and either mash or put them through a potato ricer. Add the green onions, egg yolk, salt and pepper. Mix together and form into four good-sized griddle cakes. Heat a nonstick frying pan on medium-high heat with vegetable oil or butter. Place the cakes in the pan and brown on both sides—about 5 minutes per side—then serve.

Pommes Anna

❧

2 lbs.	large baking potatoes (about 4)	1 kg
2 Tbsp.	melted butter	30 mL
2 tsp.	salt	5 mL

SERVES 4 TO 6

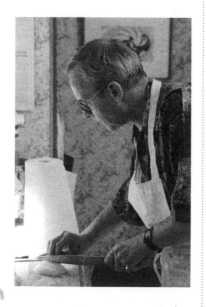

I always do this potato dish for special dinners when we have people over. It never fails to impress because it comes out looking crispy and golden brown. It portions up just like a cake.

Preheat oven to 450°F (230°C).

Peel and thinly slice potatoes (⅛ inch/3 mm) keeping each potato in a stack.

Pour half of the melted butter into a 7-inch (1.5 L) soufflé dish and begin to layer the potatoes in a circular pattern. This is easily done by simply flattening out the each stack with the palm of your hand, allowing them to overlap. Season with a pinch of salt halfway through the layering process. When all the potatoes are in place and the pan is approximately ¾ full, pour on the remaining melted butter. Tightly cover the dish with aluminum foil.

Place in hot oven and bake covered for 30 minutes. Loosen the foil lid to allow the steam to escape, seal it again, then continue baking for a further 30 minutes.

Remove from the oven and take off foil. Run a knife around the sides of the dish to loosen any potato that might have stuck to the sides. Carefully cover the dish with a serving plate and invert to unmold the potatoes.

Vegetables & Side Dishes

Artichoke Hearts
with Lemon Butter Sauce

4	medium artichokes	4
1	lemon	1
	SAUCE	
2	egg yolks	2
	juice of 1 lemon	
1 Tbsp.	white wine vinegar	15 mL
	salt	
¼ lb.	butter, melted	125 g

SERVES 4

Our kids love anything they can eat with their hands. They really enjoy dipping the artichoke leaves into the butter sauce and working their way to the best part of the artichoke heart.

Trim the sharp spikes off the ends of the artichokes by clipping with a sharp pair of scissors. Cut about ½ inch (1.5 cm) off the very top of the leaves and remove the stem. Cook in a large pot of boiling salted water to which a quartered lemon has been added (this prevents the choke from turning black). The chokes will naturally float, so a small lid or plate placed inside can be used to weigh them down as they boil. Cook like this for 20 minutes.

Test for doneness by piercing the base of the choke with a knife. If it goes in easily they are cooked.

Place upside down on a plate and drain well to release any water that is trapped in the pointed leaves.

When artichokes are drained and cool, carefully remove the very centre leaves to expose the bristly core. Using a teaspoon, carefully scrape out the bristly hairs that sit on top of the heart. This little cavity becomes the container for the dipping sauce.

SAUCE: In a stainless steel mixing bowl, whisk together the egg yolk, lemon juice, vinegar and salt. Fill a medium-sized saucepan with water and bring to a boil. Turn down the heat to medium and place the bowl with the ingredients on top of it. Whisk the mixture over the hot water until it begins to froth and thicken. (Be careful not to get the eggs too hot or they will cook and stick to the bowl.) When the eggs have thickened (this should take only 2 to 3 minutes), remove from the pot, and slowly add the melted butter. Whisk constantly until all the butter is incorporated. Check for taste. The sauce can either be served on the side, or poured into the centre of the choke.

Bon appetit!

Honey-Glazed Carrots

❧

In France this is known as Vichy Carrots and made with butter, Vichy water and sugar, but I've used honey instead. I look forward to making it with baby carrots right out of the ground. Use four baby carrots per person or, when they're not available, 1 medium carrot per person.

It's also wonderful made with winter squashes, such as acorn or butternut.

¾ lb.	sliced carrots	375 g
	salted boiling water	
1 Tbsp.	butter	15 mL
2 Tbsp.	honey	30 mL
	salt to taste	

SERVES 4

Remove green tops from the carrots, wash and scrape. Place carrots in boiling salted water and cook uncovered for approximately 5 minutes until just cooked. Remove the carrots from the boiling water and set aside.

In a medium-sized frying pan, melt the butter and honey on medium-high heat. Toss the cooked carrots in the mixture for 2 to 3 minutes to glaze them.

Baked Leeks
and Vinaigrette

2	large leeks	2
3 Tbsp.	butter	45 mL
	salt and pepper	
	VINAIGRETTE	
2 Tbsp.	white wine vinegar	30 mL
6 Tbsp.	olive oil	90 mL
	salt and pepper	
2 Tbsp.	chopped fresh parsley	30 mL

SERVES 4

The leek has long been a national symbol of the Welsh. Cooked leeks are still very popular in Wales. On Saint David's Day (the patron saint of Wales), tradition has it that you eat a raw leek. They are a wonderful ingredient because they have such natural sweetness.

Preheat oven to 350°F (180°C).

Cut off the white part of the leek and reserve the green tops for stock. Now cut the leeks lengthwise. Wash well under running water to remove any mud or sand.

Place the 4 pieces of leek centres down in a heavy baking dish. Place cubes of butter around the leeks. Season with salt and pepper. Cover the baking dish with foil and bake for 30 to 35 minutes until the leeks are very tender and you can pierce them with a fork.

VINAIGRETTE: I never measure the proportions of oil to vinegar. The guideline for most of these simple acid/oil dressings is 3 parts oil to 1 part vinegar. Once you feel comfortable making these dressings, you can vary these proportions according to your own taste or, for example, the ripeness of the tomatoes.

Combine all the ingredients in a bowl and whisk together. Pour over warm leeks and let stand at room temperature for 20 to 30 minutes.

Fresh Chanterelle Mushrooms Sautéed with Thyme and Sherry

For my friend Harry and me, this is a twice-a-year ritual dinner. In the spring we make this dish with morels and in the late summer and fall we make it with chanterelles. I like to pour it over a mound of mashed potatoes. Serve with a chilled glass of good sherry.

In a saucepan over medium heat, melt the butter and sauté the shallots and garlic until tender. Add the mushrooms and thyme, then sauté until tender. Add the sherry, chicken stock and cream. Cook for 10 to 15 minutes on medium heat until slightly thickened. Season with salt and pepper.

¼ cup	butter	50 mL
2	shallots, sliced	2
1 tsp.	minced garlic	5 mL
1 lb.	chanterelle or morel mushrooms, quartered	500 g
1 tsp.	chopped fresh thyme leaves	5 mL
½ cup	medium-dry sherry	125 mL
½ cup	chicken stock	125 mL
½ cup	heavy cream	125 mL
	pinch salt	
	freshly ground pepper	
	fresh thyme for garnish	

SERVES 4

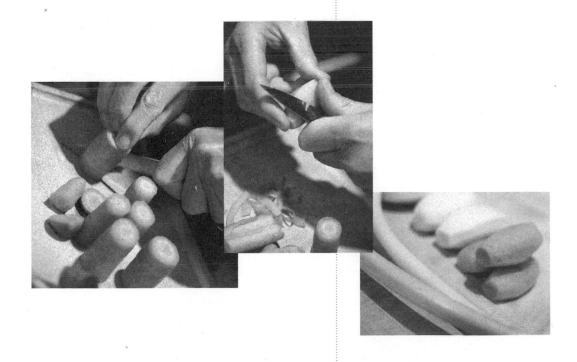

Baked Spaghetti Squash

1	medium spaghetti squash	1
½ cup	water	125 mL
2 Tbsp.	butter, melted	30 mL
	salt and pepper	

SERVES 4 TO 6

Spaghetti squash is particularly valuable to the home cook. It's simple to prepare and lighter in texture than other squashes, and it yields so much. When I prepare this unique squash for dinner I like to bake it ahead of time and then reheat it with a small amount of chicken stock just before serving.

Don't throw away the seeds. They are delicious fried in oil and salted. They can be tossed in a salad or sprinkled on soup as a savoury topping.

Preheat oven to 350°F (180°C).

Cut spaghetti squash in half lengthwise. Remove the seeds, and place cut side down on a roasting pan. Add the water and place in oven. Bake for 50 to 60 minutes, until tender.

Remove from oven and scrape the spaghetti-like flesh lengthwise with a fork to release the strands. Toss squash in melted butter and season with salt and pepper. Serve hot by itself or with Quick Tomato Sauce (page 141).

Baked Acorn Squash

Despite its simplicity—or maybe because of it—this is an unbelievably delicious way to prepare any member of the squash family, with the exception of spaghetti squash. It makes a good accompaniment to roast turkey or chicken.

Preheat oven to 350°F (180°C).

Cut ½ inch (1.5 cm) off the top and bottom of the squash. Cut the squash in half lengthwise. Scoop out the seeds and cut each half into 8 segments.

Place the squash slices in a heavy baking dish. Put cubes of butter around the squash. Sprinkle sugar, salt and allspice over and add cinnamon stick.

Cover the baking dish with foil and cook for 25 to 30 minutes. Make sure you save the roasting juices to baste the squash before serving.

1½ lb.	acorn squash	750 g
4 Tbsp.	butter	50 mL
2 Tbsp.	sugar	30 mL
½ tsp.	salt	2 mL
½ tsp.	allspice	2 mL
1	cinnamon stick	1

SERVES 6 TO 8

Baked Sweet Onions Gratinée

3	large sweet variety onions (2 lbs./1 kg)	3
2 Tbsp.	vegetable oil	30 mL
4 tsp.	Dijon mustard	25 mL
⅓ cup	cold water	75 mL
1 cup	dry breadcrumbs	250 mL
1	clove garlic, finely chopped	1
1 Tbsp.	chopped parsley	15mL
1 Tbsp.	olive oil	15mL

SERVES 6 TO 8

When shopping for onions look for Walla Walla, Maui, or better still Kelsey Giants, which are grown for us at Hazelmere Organic Farm.

This recipe was inspired by my longtime friends the Smallwoods, who prepare a similar version at their home.

Preheat oven 350°F (180°C).

Peel and cut up each onion into eight wedges, making sure to keep the root intact at the bottom of each one. Brush with vegetable oil and place in a roasting pan. Bake one side for 20 minutes then turn the onion over and bake the other side for another 20 minutes. Remove from the oven and place onions in a shallow casserole.

Whisk together the mustard and water and pour over the onions. Mix breadcrumbs, garlic, parsley and olive oil together for topping. Sprinkle over the onions and bake until the topping is light brown, approximately 15 minutes.

Sweet Onions

This dead-simple recipe makes a wonderful side dish. The onions are not browned in this preparation, just steamed very gently. Note that there is no added salt or pepper to take away from the sweetness of the onions. Even with regular white onions this method intensifies the sweetness.

2	peeled Vidalia, Walla Walla or other sweet onions	2
2 Tbsp.	butter	25 mL

SERVES 4

Cut onions into ¼-inch slices (5 mm). Place the butter and onions in a heavy medium-sized saucepan. Seal the pot with aluminum foil, then a tightly fitting lid. Place the pot over low heat and slowly cook for 45 minutes, making sure not to remove the foil or lid during the cooking process. Remove lid and foil after cooking and serve.

Curried Root Vegetables

❦

2 Tbsp.	butter	25 mL
1	clove garlic, minced	1
1	small onion cut into 1-inch (2.5 cm) dice	1
2-3 tsp.	curry powder	10-15 mL
½ tsp.	yellow mustard seeds	2 mL
3	medium carrots	3
1	yam	1
1	potato	1
3	tomatoes, roughly chopped	3
1 cup	tomato juice	250 mL
	salt	

SERVES 3 TO 4

A curry doesn't have to be hot, and this one isn't. But if you're like me and love spicy food, you can always add some Tabasco or other hot sauce to spice it up.

In a large pot, melt the butter over medium-low heat. Add garlic and onions and sauté until tender. Add curry powder and mustard seeds and cook for 2 to 3 minutes.

Peel the carrots, yam and potato and cut into 1-inch (2.5 cm) chunks. Add to onions along with tomatoes and tomato juice. Cook on low heat with the lid on for 20 to 25 minutes, until the vegetables are tender. Season with salt.

Roasted Beets

❦

2	large beets, peeled and cut in eighths	2
1 Tbsp.	vegetable oil	15 mL
½ tsp.	salt	2 mL

SERVES 4

When you roast beets, the natural sugar inside them intensifies and slightly caramelizes. They come out tasting much richer than boiled beets.

Preheat oven to 375°F (190°).

Brush beets with oil and sprinkle with salt. Place on roasting pan and bake for 25 to 30 minutes, until tender when pierced with a sharp knife. Remove from the oven and allow to cool for 5 minutes. Serve with cottage cheese on the side and slices of fresh tomato. Garnish with ground pepper and fresh dill sprigs.

Roasted Winter Vegetables with Horseradish Sauce

❦

My sister is a vegetarian and this is one of the dishes she makes. We like to serve it as part of a vegetarian dinner or as an accompaniment to meat dishes. The root vegetables all have distinctly different flavours. When roasted together with the garlic they fill the kitchen with the most wonderful aroma.

Preheat oven to 400°F (200°C).

Bring a large pot of water to a boil. Meanwhile, trim the tops of the onions and peel off the outer skin without removing the root. Cut them into quarters, leaving the root attached, to keep them together. Cut the rutabaga, parsnips and celery root into 1-inch (2.5 cm) chunks.

Put the butter and olive oil into a roasting pan and heat in the oven.

Meanwhile put the vegetables into boiling water and boil for 5 minutes. Drain the vegetables and place them in the sizzling butter and oil. Turn the vegetables so they are oiled on all sides. Bake uncovered for 15 minutes.

Break the garlic into individual cloves but do not peel. Add the garlic to the vegetables and roast for a further 20 minutes, or until they are golden brown and tender.

SAUCE: While vegetables are roasting, prepare sauce. Mix together horseradish, sour cream, lemon juice and seasonings and chill until needed.

Serve vegetables at once with lemon wedges and the sauce.

2	medium red onions	2
2	medium parsnips peeled	2
1	medium rutabaga, peeled	1
1	medium celery root peeled	1
2 Tbsp.	butter	30 mL
2 Tbsp.	olive oil	30 mL
1	head garlic	1
	lemon wedges	

SAUCE

2 tsp.	horseradish	10 mL
⅔ cup	sour cream	150 mL
	juice of ½ lemon	
	salt and freshly ground pepper	

SERVES 4

Braised Red Cabbage and Apple

🌿

1 Tbsp.	butter	15 mL
½ cup	chopped onion	125 mL
1 tsp.	fennel seeds	5 mL
4 cups	shredded red cabbage	1 L
2 Tbsp.	Ribena Blackcurrant Cordial, optional	30 mL
1 cup	apple juice	250 mL
1 tsp.	salt	5 mL
1	apple, peeled, cored, chopped	1
1	cinnamon stick	1
3 Tbsp.	vinegar	45 mL
3 Tbsp.	brown sugar	45 mL

SERVES 6

My first job after leaving hotel school was in a very famous club in Knightsbridge, London, called the Danish Club. That's where I first developed a love for Northern European food. This is one of the recipes I would prepare there. It goes great with roasted or grilled pork or poultry.

Melt butter in large pot and sauté onion and cabbage on medium heat for 5 minutes. Add all the other ingredients. Cover and slowly cook on low heat for 45 minutes, stirring occasionally to make sure the cabbage is not burning.

Asian Stir-Fry

🌿

4 Tbsp.	sesame oil	50 mL
2	carrots, peeled and thinly sliced	2
2 ribs	celery, thinly sliced	2
2	baby bok choy, washed and roughly chopped	2
8 cups	napa cabbage, sliced into ½-inch (1.5 cm) strips	2 L
2 tsp.	fresh ginger, grated	10 mL
½ tsp.	salt	2 mL

SERVES 4

I think of this as a wonderful warm vegetable salad. Cooking these ingredients very quickly is important in order to preserve all the freshness and colour. Serve it in a bowl as you would a salad.

In a large skillet or wok, heat sesame oil over medium heat. Add carrots and celery. Cover skillet and cook until tender. Remove cover and add bok choy, cabbage, grated ginger and salt. Cook quickly until cabbage is just tender yet hot.

Savoury Pies & Casseroles

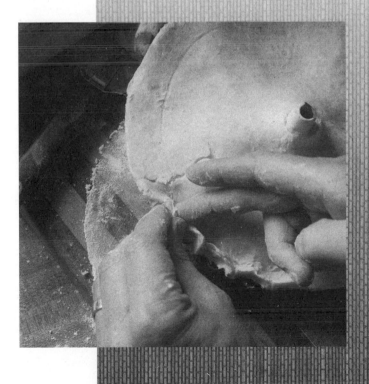

Basic Pastry

2¼ cups	flour	550 mL or 330 g
1	pinch salt	1
1 cup	butter, room temperature but not soft	250 mL
½ cup	cold water	125 mL

YIELDS ENOUGH FOR 1 DOUBLE CRUST PIE

This is a no-fail pastry recipe. Just follow the simple guidelines, the most important of which are: let the pastry rest, and don't work it too much.

Sift together flour and salt in a medium bowl. Work butter into flour with a pastry cutter and then with your hands until well blended. Add cold water and cut through with a butter knife. Carefully form into a ball by pushing the mixture together rather then working it. Cover with plastic wrap and chill in fridge for one hour.

Remove from fridge and roll out the dough on a lightly floured surface. If you only need enough for a single crust, rewrap the remainder and freeze.

Note: The butter in this pastry makes it very rich. You can substitute half of the butter for shortening, and the pastry will be equally light and flaky.

Artichoke Quiche

Theresa makes this for lunch quite often. The great thing about it is you can make it up ahead of time and then relax when your guests arrive. We always serve it with a big bowl of salad.

Preheat oven to 425°F (220°C).

Roll out pastry dough and line a 9-inch (23 cm) tart pan. Sprinkle chopped artichokes, cheese and shallots over dough. Beat eggs slightly in a bowl, then beat in remaining ingredients. Pour egg mixture into pie pan. Bake 15 minutes.

Reduce oven temperature to 300°F (150°C) and bake 30 minutes longer or until knife inserted comes out clean. Let stand 10 minutes before cutting.

½ recipe	Basic Pastry (opposite)	½ recipe
14-oz	tin artichokes, drained well and chopped	398 mL
1 cup	shredded Swiss cheese	250 mL
⅓ cup	minced shallots or onion	75 mL
4	eggs	4
2 cups	whipping cream or light cream	500 mL
¾ tsp.	salt	4 mL
¼ tsp.	sugar	1 mL
2 tsp.	minced fresh parsley	10 mL
⅛ tsp.	cayenne pepper	0.5 mL

SERVES 6

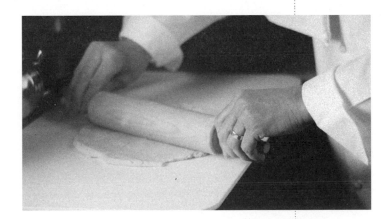

Cherry Tomato Tart

❦

½ recipe	Basic Pastry (page 60)	½ recipe
1½ cups	grated cheddar cheese	375 mL
12	cherry tomatoes, cut in half crosswise	12
2	eggs	2
⅔ cup	light cream	150 mL
	salt and freshly ground pepper	
2 Tbsp.	chopped fresh basil leaves	30 mL

SERVES 4

This light tart, sweet with fresh tomatoes and fragrant with basil, celebrates the height of summer. It is excellent as a lunchtime dish. Serve it with a steamed green vegetable, or green leaf lettuce dressed with Orange Honey Vinaigrette (page 143).

Preheat oven to 375°F (190°C).

Remove pastry from fridge and roll out on a lightly floured board. Place in a 9-inch (23 cm) tart or pie pan and trim the edges. Scatter cheese over bottom of pastry. Arrange the cherry tomatoes on top of the cheese cut side up.

Whisk the eggs with the cream and salt and pepper to taste. Pour over the cheese and tomatoes.

Bake in oven for 35 to 40 minutes, until filling is set and lightly browned. Remove from oven and sprinkle with chopped basil. Allow to sit for 5 minutes before serving.

Vegetable Cheese-Crust Pie

This is a wonderful vegetarian alternative to chicken pot pie. The oyster mushrooms are essential because of their texture and mild flavour. The leeks add sweetness, but you could substitute onion or shallot if you wished.

PASTRY: In medium bowl, work butter into flour with a pastry cutter and then with your hands until well blended. Add finely grated cheddar cheese, mixing together well with your hands. Add cold water and cut through with a butter knife. Carefully form into a ball by pushing the mixture together rather then working it. Cover with plastic wrap and chill in fridge for one hour.

FILLING: Melt butter in a large saucepan on medium heat. Add leeks, carrots and celery. Cook for about 10 minutes until tender. Add mushrooms and cook for a few more minutes. Add corn, and sprinkle the flour over the vegetables. Stir flour and vegetables together and cook the flour for a few minutes, then add the stock and cream. Cook and stir until mixture thickens. Add parsley and season with salt and pepper. Put mixture into a 10-inch (25 cm) ovenproof dish with a pie bird in the centre. (The pie bird helps keep the pastry out of the filling and it also vents the pie during cooking. If you don't have one you can substitute with an inverted egg cup and add vents in the pastry.) Set aside to cool while you roll out the pastry.

Preheat oven to 400°F (200°C). Roll out pastry to about ¼ inch (5 mm) thick. Place pastry on top of mixture. Trim edges leaving a 1-inch (2.5 cm) overhang. Turn the excess pastry under to form a neat edge. Brush beaten egg over the top to glaze. Flute edges. Any extra pastry can be used to make decorative leaves. Bake for 15 minutes. Turn oven down to 350°F (180°C) and bake for a further 20 minutes, until pastry is golden and mixture is bubbling. Serve immediately.

PASTRY

½ cup	butter	125 mL
1 cup	flour, sifted	250 mL
1 cup	finely grated cheddar cheese	250 mL
¼ cup	cold water	50 mL

FILLING

2 Tbsp.	butter	25 mL
½ cup	sliced leeks, washed, white part only	125 mL
2 cups	peeled and diced carrots (3 carrots)	500 mL
2	stalks celery, finely diced	2
1¼ cups	sliced oyster mushrooms	300 mL
1 cup	corn kernels,	250 mL
2 Tbsp.	flour	25 mL
1½ cups	chicken stock or vegetable stock	375 mL
½ cup	cream	125 mL
¼ cup	finely chopped fresh parsley	50 mL
1	egg to glaze, slightly beaten	1

SERVES 4

Braised Lamb Stew
with Rosemary Dumplings

1¼ lb.	boneless leg of lamb	625 g
	salt and pepper	
1 cup	flour	250 mL
2 Tbsp.	vegetable oil for frying	30 mL
½ cup	finely chopped onion	125 mL
½ cup	finely diced carrot	125 mL
½ cup	finely diced celery	125 mL
2	cloves garlic, chopped	2
2 Tbsp.	tomato paste	30 mL
1 cup	red wine	250 mL
1 tsp.	fennel seeds	5 mL
2 cups	stock or water	500 mL

ROSEMARY DUMPLINGS

1 cup	flour	250 mL
1 tsp.	baking powder	5 mL
½ tsp.	salt	2 mL
1 tsp.	chopped rosemary leaves	5 mL
2 Tbsp.	olive oil	30 mL
½ cup	milk	125 mL

SERVES 6

FACING PAGE
Braised Lamb Stew with
Rosemary Dumplings

This dish is comfort food. It is complete, with meat, vegetables and starch all cooked and served from one favourite casserole. It cries out for a big, dusty Rhone red wine.

If you decide to buy a leg of lamb with the bone in and debone it yourself, keep any trim and bone, as this will make a really good stock for later use (page 153).

Trim off excess sinew and fat from lamb, and cut meat into 2- or 3-inch cubes (5 or 7.5 cm). Season with salt and pepper. Dip each cube into the flour, coating all sides.

Heat a frying pan on medium-high heat and add the vegetable oil. When the oil is hot, add the lamb chunks. Sauté until all sides are sealed and browned. Remove the lamb from the pan and place it in a casserole or baking dish.

Preheat oven to 375°F (190°C).

Place the frying pan back on the burner on medium-high heat. Add the chopped vegetables and sauté for approximately 5 minutes. Add the tomato paste, red wine and fennel seeds. Stir together well, and then pour it over the lamb. Top up with water or stock. Cover the baking dish with a lid or aluminum foil, and bake for 1½ hours.

Just before stew is ready, prepare dumpling mixture.

ROSEMARY DUMPLINGS: Combine flour, baking powder, salt and rosemary in a bowl. Add the olive oil and milk. Mix together to form a soft dough. Divide the dough into six pieces.

Remove stew from oven. Taste and check seasoning. Add salt and pepper to taste. Place dumplings on top of the stew. Cover and bake for a further 15 to 20 minutes. The dumplings should be light and fluffy when they are ready.

Lentil Hot Pot

❧

Theresa often makes vegetarian dishes, and I love them because somehow they seem lighter and healthier. She makes this one two different ways, using either the fresh basil and thyme, or garam masala and cilantro. Garam masala is a very fragrant Indian spice blend that adds a lovely flavour to this dish.

This hot pot makes a complete dinner served with steamed basmati rice.

Melt butter and olive oil in a large pot on medium heat. Add shallots, garlic, celery and carrots. Sauté for 3 to 5 minutes, until vegetables are softened. Add chopped tomatoes, lentils and thyme. Cook for a few minutes. Now add stock. Season with salt and pepper. Bring to a boil, then turn down heat. Cover and simmer for approximately 45 minutes. Add fresh basil and parsley and cook uncovered for an additional 5 minutes.

The cooking time can be decreased to 20 minutes if you are preparing this dish in a pressure cooker. Stir in herbs at end of cooking, put lid back on and let sit for 5 minutes.

VARIATION: Add 1 tsp. (5 mL) garam masala (instead of basil and thyme) at the end of the cooking time, along with 2 Tbsp. (30 mL) chopped fresh cilantro (instead of the parsley).

VARIATION: Instead of lentils use the same measurement of quinoa, the grain of the ancient Incas. Reduce the cooking liquid to 2 cups (500 mL).

2 Tbsp.	butter	30 mL
2 Tbsp.	olive oil	30 mL
4	shallots or 1 large onion, peeled and chopped	4
2	cloves garlic, minced	2
1	stalk celery, chopped	1
2	medium carrots, chopped	2
2	fresh tomatoes, chopped	2
1 cup	dry brown lentils, rinsed	250 mL
1 Tbsp.	chopped fresh thyme (½ tsp./2 mL dried)	15 mL
3 cups	vegetable or chicken stock	750 mL
	salt and pepper	
¼ cup	chopped fresh basil	50 mL
¼ cup	minced fresh parsley	50 mL

SERVES 4 TO 6

FACING PAGE
Spareribs for Kids, page 109;
Spring Rolls, page 14; Beet Chips, page 13;
Parmesan Crisps, page 115;
Artichoke Hearts with Lemon Butter Sauce, page 48;
Oven Fries, page 42

Vegetable Pasties

🌿

1 recipe	Basic Pastry	1 recipe
1 Tbsp.	butter	15 mL
1 cup	diced onion	250 mL
1 cup	diced carrot (2 medium)	250 mL
½ cup	diced celery, (1 stalk)	125 mL
1½ cups	diced potato	375 mL
1½ tsp.	curry powder	7 mL
1 Tbsp.	flour	15 mL
1 cup	water	250 mL
½ cup	peas	125 mL
½ cup	corn	125 mL
1 Tbsp.	chopped fresh cilantro	15 mL
	salt and pepper	

YIELDS 24 TO 26

These are somewhat untraditional pasties, with the addition of curry and cilantro, but I never hear any complaints. They are delicious served for lunch with a salad, or are great in a lunch box. They're a big hit as appetizers too. They also freeze well. A good accompaniment for them is Nana's Piccalilli (page 148).

Prepare basic pastry. Chill in fridge for 1 hour before using.

Meanwhile prepare the filling. In a large frying pan, melt butter over medium-low heat and add onions, carrots, celery and potatoes. Cover and slowly cook until the vegetables are tender, approximately 15 minutes. Stir in curry powder and flour. Cook together for 5 minutes. Add water, peas, corn and chopped cilantro. Season with salt and pepper to taste. Gently simmer for 10 minutes uncovered, stirring to make sure mixture doesn't stick. Allow to cool.

Preheat oven to 375°F (190°C).

On a lightly floured board, divide pastry in half. Roll one ball of pastry dough to ⅛-¼ inch thick (3-5 mm). Cut out 4-inch (10 cm) circles with a pastry cutter or a large yogurt container. Combine excess pastry with remaining ball. Place one heaping teaspoon (5 mL) of the vegetable filling on each of the pastry circles. Brush the outer rim of each circle with cold water. Fold in half and seal up to form a little pocket. Prick the tops with a fork or the point of a knife. Repeat with the other ball of pastry dough. Place the pockets on a cookie sheet. Bake for 20 minutes.

Baked Eggplant Casserole

❦

This is my version of Eggplant Parmigiana. It really melts in your mouth, and it's good hot or cold. For a lighter version, use grilled eggplant instead of frying with batter.

BATTERED EGGPLANT: Beat together the cream, eggs and salt in a small bowl. Slowly whisk in the flour until completely smooth. Refrigerate for 1 hour or more. Remove from the refrigerator when needed and whisk together until smooth again. It is now ready for use.

Cut eggplant into 16 to 18 slices, ¼ inch (5 mL) thick. Dip each slice into the batter, making sure you have a good coating. Heat ¾ inch (2 cm) of vegetable oil in a deep frying pan on medium-high heat until it reaches 375°F (190°C). Place each slice separately in hot oil and fry on both sides until golden brown and crispy. Using a metal skewer or tongs, lift out each of the fried eggplant slices and place on paper towels to drain.

CASSEROLE: Preheat oven to 375°F (190°C).

Spread 1 cup (250 mL) tomato sauce to line the bottom of a 9 x 13-inch casserole dish (23 x 32.5 cm). Place 8 battered eggplant slices to form a layer. Spread half of the béchamel sauce over top, then 1 cup (250 mL) tomato sauce. Sprinkle 2 Tbsp. (30 mL) Parmesan cheese. Layer remaining eggplant slices. Add the rest of the béchamel sauce and the remaining tomato sauce. Finish off with remaining Parmesan and a scattering of fresh herbs.

Bake for 35 to 40 minutes, until golden brown and bubbling.

BATTERED EGGPLANT		
2 cups	light cream	500 mL
2	whole eggs	2
½ tsp.	salt	2 mL
2¼ cups	flour	550 mL
1	large eggplant	1
	oil for frying	

CASSEROLE		
3 cups	Quick Tomato Sauce (page 141)	750 mL
2 cups	Béchamel Sauce (page 140)	500 mL
½ cup	grated Parmesan cheese	125 mL
1 Tbsp.	chopped fresh basil or oregano	15 mL

SERVES 6

Vegetarian Lasagne

3 cups	Quick Tomato Sauce (page 141)	750 mL
2 cups	Béchamel Sauce (page 140)	500 mL
2 Tbsp.	olive oil	30 mL
½	medium onion, chopped	½
1	clove garlic, minced	1
⅔ lb.	chopped fresh spinach or 1-300 g pkg. frozen, thawed and well squeezed	350 g
1 lb.	ricotta cheese	500 g
2 cups	grated mozzarella cheese	500 mL
2 tsp.	finely chopped fresh marjoram or basil	10 mL
	salt and pepper	
9	sheets oven-ready lasagne noodles	9
1 cup	grated fresh Parmesan cheese	250 mL

SERVES 8

This is a vegetarian dish, but you could add slices of grilled chicken breast as another layer. You'll probably have leftovers. It makes a lot. Anything that remains can be cut into portions and frozen for later use.

Prepare Quick Tomato Sauce and Béchamel Sauce in advance.

Heat oil in small saucepan over medium heat and add chopped onion and garlic. Cover and cook until transparent.

In medium bowl, combine spinach, ricotta cheese, half the mozzarella cheese, onion mixture, marjoram or basil and salt and pepper to taste.

Preheat oven to 350°F (180°C).

Using a 9 x 13-inch baking pan (23 x 32.5 cm), start layering the ingredients beginning with ⅓ of the tomato sauce, ⅓ of the béchamel sauce, then 3 lasagne noodles, ½ of the spinach mixture, then ⅓ of the remaining mozzarella cheese. Then layer ⅓ of the tomato sauce, ⅓ of the béchamel sauce, 3 lasagne noodles, ½ of the spinach mixture. Top with 3 more lasagne noodles. Now add the last of the tomato sauce and the remaining béchamel sauce and mozzarella cheese. Add an additional sprinkling of Parmesan cheese on top.

Cover and bake for 45 to 50 minutes. Bake an additional 10 minutes uncovered. Let stand 10 minutes before serving.

Baked Manicotti

This baked pasta dish is one that our children love. And if you make the Quick Tomato Sauce in advance, it takes very little time. I use homemade tomato sauce because it is lighter and sweeter tasting.

Prepare Quick Tomato Sauce.

Cook the manicotti shells following the package directions. Drain and rinse under cold water. Lay on a towel.

Preheat oven to 375°F (190°C).

In a large bowl, mix together the ricotta cheese, egg yolks, Parmesan cheese, Jack cheese and seasonings. Fill each of the manicotti with the filling. Place half of the tomato sauce on the bottom of a baking dish. Lay the manicotti on top. Add the remaining tomato sauce. Sprinkle with the ½ cup (125 mL) grated Parmesan cheese. Cover with foil and bake for 40 minutes.

3 cups	Quick Tomato Sauce (page 141)	750 mL
10	manicotti shells	10
1½ cups	ricotta cheese	375 mL
2	egg yolks	2
¼ cup	grated Parmesan cheese	50 mL
¼ cup	grated Jack cheese	50 mL
4 tsp.	chopped fresh marjoram	20 mL
½ tsp.	nutmeg	2 mL
½ tsp.	salt	2 mL
¼ tsp.	freshly ground pepper	1 mL
½ cup	grated Parmesan cheese, for the top	125 mL

SERVES 4 TO 5

Chicken and Vegetable Pasta Casserole

✤

1 lb.	package fusilli	500 g
2	large chicken breast halves, boned and skinned	2
2 cups	water for poaching chicken	500 mL
3 Tbsp.	olive oil	45 mL
1	onion, chopped	1
2	cloves garlic, minced	2
1 cup	peeled and thinly sliced carrots	250 mL
½ cup	diced celery	125 mL
1 cup	cauliflower, broken up into small pieces	250 mL
2 cups	seeded and sliced red pepper (1 large pepper)	500 mL
1 cup	corn kernels	250 mL
2 cups	sliced mushrooms	500 mL
1 cup	sliced snow peas	250 mL
¼ cup	chopped fresh basil	50 mL
1 cup	grated Parmesan cheese	250 mL
1 cup	grated Swiss cheese	250 mL
2 tsp.	salt	10 mL
½ tsp.	cracked black pepper	2 mL
	WHITE SAUCE	
3 Tbsp.	butter	50 mL
4 Tbsp.	unbleached flour	65 mL
3 cups	milk	750 mL
	salt and pepper	
	reserved poaching liquid	

SERVES 6 TO 8

We started making take-out casseroles on request at the restaurant for customers going out on boats for the day. A casserole is a complete meal. It makes up well in advance, and it's portable and easy to freeze.

A vegetarian version of this dish would be to omit the chicken and add 2 cups of vegetable stock instead of the poaching liquid.

In a large pot of boiling water, cook pasta 8 to 10 minutes until just done (al dente). Drain and rinse under cold water. Set aside.

In shallow pan of simmering water, poach the chicken breast uncovered 10 to 15 minutes. Remove chicken from water, skim off any foam and reserve the poaching liquid. Set aside.

While chicken is simmering, start to prepare white sauce.

WHITE SAUCE: Melt butter in heavy saucepan. Add the flour and cook gently, stirring constantly until the flour is well incorporated.

Remove the butter and flour mixture from heat and pour in the milk. Return the pan to medium heat and bring the sauce to a gentle boil, stirring constantly for 5 minutes. Season to taste with salt and pepper. Add reserved poaching liquid Stir to combine and set aside.

Preheat oven to 350°F (180°C).

Heat a large frying pan on medium-high heat, add the olive oil and sauté the onion, garlic, carrot and celery for 5 minutes. Add the peppers, corn, mushrooms, cauliflower and snow peas and cook until tender for 5 to 10 minutes. Cut up the chicken breasts into bite-sized pieces.

In a large bowl combine the pasta, chicken, cooked vegetables, basil, cheese and salt and pepper.

Now mix in the white sauce. Pour into an oiled 10-by-15-inch baking dish (25 by 30 cm). Cover with aluminium foil and bake for 45 minutes.

It is nice to add a scatter of freshly chopped parsley or basil when serving.

Baked Blanket Chicken

2 cups	large-diced squash,	500 mL
1½ cups	chopped white onions	375 mL
2 cups	chopped yellow pepper	500 mL
2 cups	chopped red bell pepper	500 mL
3 cups	diced ripe tomatoes	750 mL
1 Tbsp.	olive oil	15 mL
1 whole	free-range chicken, deboned	1 whole
2 tsp.	Dijon mustard	10 mL
2 Tbsp.	olive oil	30 mL
1 tsp.	ground cumin	5 mL
	salt and pepper	
2 Tbsp.	finely chopped fresh oregano	30 mL
	juice of ½ lemon	
4 cups	dried broad egg noodles	1 L
1 Tbsp.	finely chopped fresh parsley for garnish	15 mL
1	lemon for garnish	1

SERVES 4

This is a great family meal because it's all prepared in one dish. The chicken and vegetables together create a wonderful sweet sauce. Deboning the chicken in advance makes it so easy to serve once it is roasted. Save the bones to make stock (page 152), which you can either use immediately or freeze.

You can also use 4 boneless chicken breast halves in place of the whole chicken. Simply flatten them with the smooth side of a meat tenderizer to even out the thickness.

Preheat oven to 375°F (190°C).

Place all of the vegetables in a 2½-inch-deep (6.5 cm) heavy roasting pan. Season with salt and freshly ground pepper to taste. Add 1 Tbsp. (15 mL) olive oil and toss together. Pat down to make it all even.

Place the deboned whole chicken on top of the vegetables skin side up. Brush the skin with a mixture of the mustard, 2 Tbsp. olive oil and cumin, and season with salt and pepper to taste. Sprinkle with chopped oregano and the juice of half a lemon.

Bake in oven for 1¼ hours until cooked and golden brown. Toward the end of cooking, boil the noodles and drain. Remove the chicken and toss the vegetables with the precooked noodles. Place the chicken back on top and continue to bake for a further 10 minutes until the noodles are heated through.

Cut the chicken into four pieces. Serve the pasta and vegetables in a bowl with the chicken on top. Garnish with freshly chopped parsley and large lemon wedges.

HOW TO DEBONE A CHICKEN: Lay the whole chicken on a clean chopping board, breast side down. First cut a deep slit down the back of the chicken from the neck to the tail. With a small knife, scrape and cut the meat from the bones working one side at a time. Pull the meat away with your fingers as you slowly work your way down the side of the bird. When you reach the ball joints at the legs and wings, sever them and continue on. Repeat this process on both sides until only the leg and wing bones remain. Remove the leg bones by cutting open the thighs and drumsticks to expose them. When this is complete, pat the chicken dry with paper towels and store in the refrigerator until required. Wash the cutting board and knife immediately.

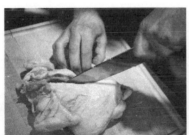

Chicken Pot Pie

It was a real treat when Mum made us a pot pie. My own children look forward to it as well. It's great served hot with a crisp salad as a contrast.

Quite often we make this dish using leftover roast chicken or turkey. You can use a combination of chicken stock and cream, or if you don't have any chicken stock on hand you can also make the sauce simply with 2 cups (500 mL) of milk.

½ recipe	Basic Pastry (page 60)	½ recipe
1 lb.	chicken breast and/or legs	500 g
4 cups	cold water	1 L
3 Tbsp.	butter	45 mL
1 cup	diced onions	250 mL
½ cup	diced celery (1 stalk)	125 mL
1 cup	diced carrots	250 mL
¾ cup	thinly sliced leek, white part only	175 mL
3 Tbsp.	flour	45 mL
2 cups	poaching liquid (for a richer sauce: 1½ cups/375 mL poaching liquid and ½ cup/125 mL cream)	500 mL
½ cup	peas	125 mL
½ cup	corn	125 mL
1 Tbsp.	finely chopped fresh thyme leaves	15 mL
2 Tbsp.	finely chopped fresh parsley	30 mL
1 tsp.	salt	5 mL
½ tsp.	freshly ground black pepper	2 mL

SERVES 4 TO 6

Prepare pastry dough and cool in fridge for at least an hour.

Place the chicken in 4 cups (1 L) of cold water and bring to a simmer. Poach boneless chicken breast for 20 minutes and chicken legs for 35 minutes. Remove the chicken from the heat and strain, reserving the poaching liquid, as you will need it to make the sauce. Cube the chicken.

In a large pot, melt the butter and add the onion, celery, carrot and leek. Sauté for 10 minutes until vegetables are tender. Add the flour and cook for a few more minutes stirring constantly to incorporate and cook the flour. Add 2 cups (500 mL) of the poaching liquid. Stir and simmer for 10 minutes until the sauce has thickened. If you have chosen to make a rich sauce, with ½ cup (125 mL) of cream, add this at the end of the cooking process.

Preheat oven to 350°F (180°C).

Now add the peas, corn and cubed chicken to the sauce. Season with the chopped thyme, parsley and salt and pepper. Pour into a deep 10-inch (25 cm) pie dish. Place a pie bird in the centre of the dish. The pie bird helps keep the pastry out of the filling and it also vents the pie during cooking. If you don't have one you can substitute with an inverted egg cup. Set aside to cool while you roll out the pastry.

Roll out the pastry and place on top of the pie. Trim the edges. Brush with beaten egg or milk to glaze. Remaining pastry can be used to decorate top of pie with leaves or other shapes. Cut 4 small vents in the pastry to allow steam to escape. Bake for 40 to 45 minutes.

Salmon on the Barbecue in Foil / 76

Poached Salmon Steaks with Dill Caper Sauce / 77

Grilled Salmon with Sesame Glaze and Wild Rice Pancake / 78

Roasted Halibut with Sweet Corn Relish / 80

Baked Fillets of Halibut with Black Bean Glaze / 81

Roasted Cod with Lemon Breadcrumbs / 82

Tuna Steak with Tomato, Mushroom and Black Olive Sauce / 83

Salmon and Shrimp Cakes with Blueberry Pear Salsa / 84

Asian Prawn Brochette / 85

Black Thai Rice with Prawns and Ginger / 86

Dungeness Crab and Eggplant Cannelloni / 87

Steamed Clams / 88

Fanny Bay Baked Oysters / 89

Stuffed Squid / 90

Fish & Shellfish

Salmon on the Barbecue in Foil

1 side	salmon, filleted (approximately 3 lbs./1.5 kg)	1 side
2 Tbsp.	olive oil	30 mL
2 Tbsp.	chopped chives	30 mL
1	shallot, thinly sliced	1
1	clove garlic, minced	1
2 Tbsp.	chopped fresh dill	30 mL
½ tsp.	salt	2 mL
	cracked black pepper	
2 Tbsp.	dried herbes de Provence	30 mL
½ cup	white wine	125 mL

SERVES 6

My friend Gerald Smallwood, an ex-marine engineer who repaired fish boats up the coast, first showed me how to prepare this dish. He makes it on a barbecue but it also works well in the oven.

It makes a nice centrepiece for a summer buffet because it can be served hot or cold. Serve it with boiled new potatoes and lots of lemon wedges.

Preheat oven to 400°F (200°C), or light barbecue.

Scale salmon and remove fine bones. Place side of salmon on a double layer of foil. Rub salmon with olive oil. Sprinkle with chives, shallot, garlic, dill, salt and pepper. Add herbes de Provence.

Pull up the edges of the foil to form an envelope. Pour in the white wine and seal the foil well. Bake for 25 to 30 minutes.

Poached Salmon Steaks
with Dill Caper Sauce

I like to use salmon steaks because fish cooked on the bone always tastes better. You can use this recipe for halibut steaks as well. If you have a proper fish poacher it will be easier to move the fish in and out of the poaching liquid. This dish can be served hot or just warm.

SAUCE: Make up 1 recipe of béchamel sauce. Add the white wine, dill and whole capers. Bring to simmer on medium heat. Season to taste with a small amount of freshly ground pepper. You usually don't need to add salt to this sauce because the capers are fairly salty. Cover the surface of the sauce with lightly buttered parchment paper and keep warm. Now prepare the salmon.

Place the wine, water, vegetables, bay leaf and lemon slices in a large skillet or fish poacher. Bring to a simmer on medium-high heat. Add the salmon steaks so the fish is completely immersed in the cooking liquid. Cover and simmer gently on medium heat for 5 minutes. Remove pan from the heat and let the fish rest in the liquid for a further 5 minutes, uncovered.

Transfer the salmon steaks onto a large warmed platter. Quickly but carefully remove the skin and bone from each steak. This makes them easier to eat.

To serve, ladle equal portions of sauce onto warm plates. Place salmon on top of sauce. Garnish with sprigs of fresh dill.

	SAUCE	
2 cups	Béchamel Sauce (page 140)	500 mL
½ cup	dry white wine	125 mL
2 Tbsp.	finely chopped fresh dill	25 mL
1 Tbsp.	capers, rinsed and drained	15 mL
	freshly ground pepper to taste	
2 cups	dry white wine	500 mL
2 cups	cold water	500 mL
1	medium carrot, thinly sliced	1
½	medium onion, thinly sliced	½
1	rib celery, thinly sliced	1
1	bay leaf	1
2	lemon slices	2
4	salmon steaks, centre cut (1½ lbs./750 g)	4
4	sprigs fresh dill for garnish	4

SERVES 4

Grilled Salmon with Sesame Glaze and Wild Rice Pancake

❧

	SALMON	
1 cup	soy sauce	250 mL
½ cup	brown sugar	125 mL
1 cup	water	250 mL
¼ cup	sesame oil	50 mL
1 Tbsp.	minced ginger	15 mL
1 Tbsp.	cornstarch	15 mL
2 Tbsp.	cold water	30 mL
2 lbs.	salmon fillets	1 kg
	vegetable oil for fillets	
	salt and pepper	
1 Tbsp.	toasted sesame seeds for garnish	15 mL
2 Tbsp.	cilantro leaves for garnish	30 mL

SERVES 6

This glaze was inspired by a trip to Alaska where we caught and had salmon barbecued by a Native fish guide who marinated it in a similar way.

This is the one salmon dish we serve all summer at the restaurant. It is a real hit with out-of-town guests, especially when served with Chef Dennis Green's wild rice pancakes.

If you barbecue the fillets in a wire basket, it makes flipping the fish easier and prevents sticking.

SALMON: Combine soy sauce, brown sugar, 1 cup (250 mL) water, sesame oil and ginger and bring to a boil over medium-high heat. Combine cornstarch and 2 Tbsp. (30 mL) cold water in small bowl. Blend well and add to pot. Stir until mixture is thickened, about 5 minutes, and then strain. Keep warm until needed.

Brush salmon fillets with a small amount of vegetable oil and season with salt and pepper. Grill on barbecue over high heat until just done, 3 to 5 minutes each side.

PANCAKES: Wash the rice thoroughly. Combine rice with the water in a small heavy saucepan. Bring to a boil, then immediately reduce heat to low. Cover with a tight-fitting lid and simmer for 40 minutes. Remove from heat and drain any excess water. Allow to cool.

Combine flour, baking powder, salt and sugar in a bowl and set aside. In a large mixing bowl whisk eggs and then add milk and melted butter. Mix the dry ingredients into the wet ingredients and stir until well blended. Add the rice, carrots, celery, chives and parsley. Stir to form a chunky batter. Ladle out ¼ cup (50 mL) portions onto a hot, lightly oiled nonstick frying pan or griddle iron and cook until nice and brown in colour. Turn and cook about 2 minutes longer on the other side. To keep warm, place parchment paper between layers and place in 200°F (95°C) oven. This recipe will make 12 to 14 pancakes.

To serve, place 2 pancakes on a warm plate. Lay grilled salmon on top. Then lightly top with the sesame ginger glaze. Garnish with toasted sesame seeds and chopped fresh cilantro leaves.

PANCAKES		
½ cup	wild rice, uncooked	125 mL
1½ cups	cold water	375 mL
1 cup	flour	250 mL
1½ tsp.	baking powder	7 mL
1 tsp.	salt	5 mL
1½ tsp.	sugar	7 mL
2	eggs	2
¾ cup	milk	175 mL
2 Tbsp.	melted butter	30 mL
½ cup	grated carrot	125 mL
½ cup	finely diced celery	125 mL
1 Tbsp.	chopped chives	15 mL
1 Tbsp.	chopped parsley	15 mL

SERVES 6

Roasted Halibut
with Sweet Corn Relish

❦

Halibut season starts around March and goes right through until the fall. This is a very versatile fish, but I like to prepare it quite simply, so that you can enjoy the natural fresh flavour.

At the restaurant, because we cook individual portions most of the time, we use shallow aluminum plates for roasting. These are great for one or two portions and help make the cleanup easier after dinner. You can find them at restaurant supply stores or East Indian food stores.

HALIBUT: Preheat oven to 375°F (190°C). Cut four 5-inch (12.5 cm) squares of parchment paper.

Season the halibut with salt, pepper and paprika. Brush with vegetable oil and place each steak on a piece of parchment and then on a shallow baking sheet.

Roast for approximately 15 minutes. Remove fish from the oven and serve with the relish.

SWEET CORN RELISH: Blanch the corn on the cob in boiling water for 5 minutes. Drain and plunge into cold water. Remove corn from cob with a sharp knife.

Place corn and remaining ingredients in a large pot. Bring to a boil, then simmer uncovered for 25 minutes. Let cool. Pour into clean container. Keeps refrigerated for 2 weeks.

In the fall, when corn is in season, it's a good idea to make lots of this and preserve it. Immediately after cooking, pour hot relish into sterilized sealing jars. Place sterilized lids on top and secure with rings. Follow manufacturer's instructions for sterilizing jars and lids.

HALIBUT

4 6-oz.	halibut steaks, boneless and skinless	4 175 g
3 Tbsp.	vegetable oil	45 mL
	salt and pepper	
	pinch mild paprika	

SERVES 4

SWEET CORN RELISH

4-5	fresh corn cobs (2 ½ cups/625 mL kernels)	4-5
1 cup	white wine vinegar	250 mL
¾ cup	white sugar	175 mL
¼ cup	finely chopped white onion	50 mL
¼ cup	diced red pepper	50 mL
¼ cup	diced green pepper	50 mL
¼ cup	diced celery	50 mL
¼ cup	water	50 mL
2 tsp.	dry mustard	10 mL
½ tsp.	celery seed	2 mL
½ tsp.	mustard seed	2 mL
½ tsp.	salt	2 mL
¼ tsp.	chili flakes	1 mL

YIELDS 3 CUPS (750 mL)

Baked Fillets of Halibut with Black Bean Glaze

❧

This easy weeknight recipe uses a commercially prepared black bean sauce which can be found in the Asian section of your supermarket. It can be used as a simple glaze for other white fish, such as red snapper or cod. This dish is great served with plain steamed rice or noodles and Chinese greens such as bok choy or Chinese cabbage.

Preheat oven to 400°F. (200°C).

Place fillets on baking sheet that is lined with parchment paper. This prevents sticking. Mix together the black bean sauce, soy sauce, sesame oil and ginger. Lightly brush the top of the fish with the glaze. Bake for 15 to 20 minutes until fish is opaque all through. Remove from oven, sprinkle with chopped green onion and serve.

VARIATION: Instead of roasting, steam the glazed fish for the same length of time.

4 7-oz.	halibut fillets	4 200 g
4 tsp.	black bean sauce	20 mL
2 tsp.	soy sauce	10 mL
1 tsp.	sesame oil	5 mL
1 tsp.	peeled, grated fresh ginger	5 mL
1	green onion, chopped	1

SERVES 4

Roasted Cod
with Lemon Breadcrumbs

❧

1½ cups	fresh white breadcrumbs	375 mL
6 Tbsp.	chopped fresh parsley	90 mL
2 tsp.	lemon zest	10 mL
3 Tbsp.	butter or olive oil	45 mL
	salt and pepper	
1½ lbs.	cod steaks	750 g

SERVES 4

This is a very simple and easy way to coat and cook fresh firm white fish. You may prefer to use olive oil for an even lighter flavour.

Preheat oven to 400°F (200°C).

Mix together fresh breadcrumbs, parsley and lemon zest in a medium bowl. Place butter or olive oil in the roasting pan and heat in the oven.

Season cod with salt and pepper.

Remove pan from oven and tip slightly so the butter or oil pools at one end. Dip cod into melted butter to coat thoroughly, then into breadcrumb mixture. Cover completely with crumbs. Arrange pieces on roasting dish allowing a small amount of space around each one. Bake for 18 to 20 minutes until brown and cooked.

Tuna Steak with Tomato, Mushroom and Black Olive Sauce

At the restaurant we like to let people know that we serve tuna rare. Try to buy the best quality tuna. Ask for sashimi grade, and then don't overcook it, or it will dry out.

This makes for a spectacular presentation when it's served with Black Olive and Crunchy Garlic Mashed Potatoes (page 44). Rapini or winter kale is a great complement.

SAUCE: Place a saucepan on medium high heat. Add olive oil and sliced mushrooms, cover and cook until mushrooms are tender. Now add tomato and olives. Cook for 5 to 10 minutes. Set aside.

Brush the tuna steaks with oil and season with salt and pepper. Place a frying pan on medium-high heat. Sear steaks 3 to 4 minutes per side for rare. When the tuna is browned on both sides, remove from heat and serve immediately.

Place a mound of mashed potatoes on warmed plate. Then place the seared tuna on top of the potatoes. Top the tuna with the Tomato, Mushroom and Olive Sauce. Garnish with chopped cilantro or parsley.

SAUCE

2 Tbsp.	olive oil	30 mL
2-3	shiitake mushrooms, sliced	2-3
1	large fresh ripe tomato, blanched, seeded and chopped	1
2 Tbsp.	coarsely chopped pitted black olives	30 mL
1 Tbsp.	chopped cilantro, or Italian flat-leaf parsley for garnish	15 mL
	salt and pepper	

TUNA

2 6-oz.	tuna steaks, 1-1½-inch (2.5-4 cm) thick	2 175 g
1 Tbsp.	vegetable oil	15 mL
	salt and freshly ground pepper	

SERVES 2

Salmon and Shrimp Cakes with Blueberry Pear Salsa

❦

¾ lb.	salmon fillet	350 g
	salt and pepper	
	vegetable oil	
½ lb.	baby shrimp, peeled	250 g
2 Tbsp.	fresh parsley, chopped	30 mL
1 cup	fresh breadcrumbs	250 mL
½ cup	light mayonnaise	125 mL
½ tsp.	freshly grated pepper	2 mL
1	green onion, chopped	1
2 Tbsp.	vegetable oil	30 mL
1 tsp.	finely grated lemon zest	5 mL
½ cup	cornmeal	125 mL
½ cup	flour	125 mL

YIELDS 4 CAKES

BLUEBERRY PEAR SALSA

2 Tbsp.	chopped cilantro	30 mL
3 Tbsp.	finely diced red onion	45 mL
1	ripe pear, peeled, cored and diced (½ cup/125 mL)	1
1 cup	fresh blueberries, cleaned	250 mL
2 Tbsp.	fresh lime juice	30 mL
	pinch of salt	

YIELDS 2 CUPS (500 mL)

Traditional fish cakes have come a long way. They used to be made from leftover fish and mashed potatoes. Now we make them with a whole variety of fresh ingredients. The salmon gives a nice rich quality to these cakes and the shrimps add sweetness. You can use other types of fish, such as halibut. We like to serve the cakes with salsa made with seasonal fruit, or even tropical fruit, like mangoes. The possibilities are endless.

Season salmon fillet with salt and pepper and rub with a small amount of vegetable oil. Pan sear or barbecue 10 minutes per side. Set aside to cool.

Flake salmon fillet into small chunks and place in a large bowl. To make fresh breadcrumbs, chop bread in food processor for a few minutes until fine crumbs are formed. Add to bowl along with the shrimp and all the remaining ingredients except cornmeal and flour. Combine mixture well and divide into 4 portions. Form these portions into cakes. Combine cornmeal and flour and dip fishcakes in, making sure to pat the coating onto the cakes well.

Preheat nonstick frying pan on medium heat. Add oil and cakes and gently brown for approximately 10 minutes per side until completely warmed through and lightly browned.

BLUEBERRY PEAR SALSA: In a bowl combine all ingredients. Mix well and let stand for about 2 hours in the refrigerator so the flavours can blend together.

Asian Prawn Brochette

In this recipe we are using fresh ginger root. A few years ago one of my Asian customers tore a strip off me for using chopped ginger, and later on presented me with my first ginger grater. From that day on, whenever I make a dish that calls for grated ginger I think of her and that moment. These graters are not only inexpensive, but you will find them indispensable. Unlike cheese graters, they are solid with small bumps that separate the strings from the flesh. They are made of either metal or ceramic.

Peel the prawn tails and place in a glass or stainless steel dish. Add garlic, ginger, teriyaki, hoisin or oyster sauce and lime juice. Toss together well. Cover and refrigerate for 2 hours.

Just prior to cooking, remove the prawns from the marinade. For each brochette use two parallel large wooden skewers. This prevents the prawns from flopping around when you turn them. Skewer the prawns and brush with sesame oil. Barbecue or broil for 5 minutes each side until they turn pink.

To serve, garnish with fresh cilantro leaves and wedges of lime.

30	prawn tails, peeled	30
1	clove garlic, chopped	1
1 tsp.	grated ginger root	5 mL
1 Tbsp.	teriyaki sauce	15 mL
1 Tbsp.	hoisin or oyster sauce	15 mL
	juice of 1 lime	
2 Tbsp.	sesame oil	30 mL
1 Tbsp.	chopped cilantro leaves	15 mL
	lime wedges for garnish	

SERVES 4

Black Thai Rice
with Prawns and Ginger

1 cup	black Thai rice/jade rice	250 mL
1 Tbsp.	butter	15 mL
½ cup	chopped onion	125 mL
1½ tsp.	grated fresh ginger	7 mL
3 cups	chicken or vegetable stock	750 mL
1 cup	uncooked prawn tails	250 mL
1 Tbsp.	chopped fresh cilantro	15 mL
1	lime, quartered	1

SERVES 4

This exotic Asian variety of rice, also known as jade rice, is grown in Northern Thailand. It reminds me of our own native wild rice—even when it is cooked it still has a crunch to it. The black colour contrasts beautifully with things like prawns or chicken.

Wash the rice under cold running water until water runs clear. Soak rice for 20 minutes in cold water. Drain and set aside.

Place the butter and chopped onions in a heavy frying pan or soup pot, cover and cook until the onions are transparent. Add the rice and ginger. Fry together for 2 to 3 minutes to allow the rice to soak up some of the butter. Pour in the stock, cover and cook on low heat for approximately 30 minutes, stirring occasionally to make sure rice is not sticking or burning.

Remove lid and add the peeled prawn tails and chopped cilantro. Stir in and cook for a further 15 minutes.

Serve garnished with fresh lime wedges.

Dungeness Crab
and Eggplant Cannelloni

❧

This is simply delicious. It's one of Chef Dennis Green's creations from the restaurant, which I prepare at home quite often. We sometimes use the filling as stuffing for homemade ravioli as well.

The trick to these ingenious eggplant cannelloni is to make sure that you slice the eggplant into thin enough slices so that it really does take the place of pasta. Look for male eggplants because they have fewer seeds than the female. The males have flat bottoms and the females have dimpled bottoms. (No comment.)

Cut eggplant in half lengthwise and cut 12 very thin slices (⅛ inch/3 mm) from the centre. Sprinkle with salt and place on paper towel to drain. Dice remaining eggplant into ¼-inch (5 mm) cubes; sprinkle with salt and place in a strainer over a bowl to drain. After 30 minutes, rinse excess salt from diced eggplant and set aside. Lightly oil and grill eggplant slices until tender, then set aside to cool.

Melt butter in medium pan and sauté shallots and diced eggplant until softened. Add garlic and continue to cook until fragrant. Stir in mascarpone cheese, allow to melt and remove from heat. Stir in parsley and crabmeat and correct seasoning. Cool.

Preheat oven to 400°F (200°C).

Once filling is cold, lay out 2 slices of grilled eggplant, overlapping slightly. Spoon ½ cup (125 mL) of filling on one edge of eggplant and roll up lengthwise to form a cannelloni shape. Place on parchment paper on a small baking sheet and bake for 10 minutes.

Serve on a pool of Tomato Red Pepper Coulis.

TOMATO RED PEPPER COULIS: Heat oil and sauté peppers and onion until softened. Add tomatoes and sherry and simmer for 20 minutes. Add cream, simmer 10 minutes longer. Purée and strain. Season to taste.

1	large eggplant	1
	salt	
2 Tbsp.	butter	30 mL
½ cup	diced shallots	125 mL
1 tsp.	minced garlic	5 mL
½ cup	mascarpone cheese or cream cheese mixed with a little cream	125 mL
1 Tbsp.	chopped parsley	15 mL
1 lb.	fresh crabmeat	500 g

TOMATO RED PEPPER COULIS

1 Tbsp.	olive oil	15 mL
1	red pepper, seeded and sliced	1
2	small red onions, sliced	2
4	ripe roma tomatoes, sliced	4
½ cup	dry sherry	125 mL
½ cup	whipping cream	125 mL
	salt and pepper to taste	

SERVES 6

Steamed Clams

❦

3-4 lbs.	small Manila clams (130-150)	1.5-2 kg
2 Tbsp.	butter	30 mL
2 Tbsp.	parsley	30 mL
2	large garlic cloves, chopped	2
1 cup	dry white wine	250 mL

SERVES 6

This is one of the first dishes I prepare when we arrive on Hornby Island for our annual family vacation. The kids get a kick out of using the empty clamshell as an implement for removing the meat from other clams.

If you need to purge the clams of sand, soak them overnight in a bucket of cold fresh water.

Rinse the clams in cold running water. Check to make sure they are all closed tight and none are full of sand. Place the butter, parsley and garlic in a large stockpot on medium-high heat. Cover and cook for 2 to 3 minutes then add the wine and clams. Cover and steam for 5 minutes or just until the clam shells open up. Serve in soup bowls with the Big Dipper Toasts (page 116).

VARIATION: This recipe can be used to make the famous Italian dish Linguine Vongole, simply by tossing the cooked clams and sauce together with the lightly cooked linguine.

Baked Fanny Bay Oysters

I love small fresh oysters served raw on the half shell, but I also like these large local briny oysters for roasting. They are exported all year round from Fanny Bay or Oyster Jim's on Vancouver Island. If you can't find either of these brand names, look for oysters at least 5 inches (12 cm) long.

Shuck the oysters, keeping the juices to use in the final sauce. Reserve the deeper side of the shells to bake the oysters in.

Preheat oven to 375°F (190°).

Place butter in a saucepan. When melted, add sliced mushrooms. Cover and cook on medium heat until softened. Add flour and cook until it is well incorporated. Remove from heat and add milk. Return to heat and stir until thickened. Now add oyster juice and white wine. Mix together, heat and cook for 5 minutes. Season with salt and pepper.

Cut up each oyster into 3 large pieces. Place back in the shells, making sure there aren't any bits of shell included by accident. Cover with 2 Tbsp. (30 mL) of sauce each. Bake on the middle rack of the oven for approximately 30 minutes or until golden brown.

4	large roasting oysters in the shell	4
2 Tbsp.	butter	30 mL
2	large shiitake or white mushrooms, sliced	2
1 Tbsp.	flour	15 mL
1 cup	milk	250 mL
2 Tbsp.	dry white wine	30 mL
	salt and pepper	

SERVES 4

Stuffed Squid

3 lbs.	squid (12 pieces)	1.5 kg
3 cups	fresh fine breadcrumbs	750 mL
3	sprigs parsley, chopped	3
3	cloves garlic, finely chopped	3
3 Tbsp.	olive oil	45 mL
	salt and pepper	
2 Tbsp.	vegetable oil for searing	30 mL
2	ripe tomatoes, skinned, de-seeded and chopped	2
1 cup	dry white wine	250 mL
2 Tbsp.	chopped fresh parsley	30 mL
1 tsp.	mild paprika	5 mL

SERVES 6

I don't make this often, but hardly a month goes by that I don't think I should make it as a treat for myself. I have had heated debates with Abel, my Portuguese friend and Bishop's restaurant manager, as to who has the better recipe. However, he doesn't have a cookbook and I do, so you get mine.

Cleaning and trimming the squid can be a real task if you haven't attempted it before. Help is at hand—cleaned squid is now readily available. But, back to the task before us. Usually squid is frozen in 3 pound (1.5 kg) blocks. Defrost the block in your refrigerator, double wrapped in plastic bags so it doesn't leak.

When defrosted, pull out the head and tentacles along with a lot of the squid's insides. Set aside the head and tentacles. Lay the squid on a board and scrape off the purplish membrane on the outside. Scrape from the pointed end to the opening, reserving the white flesh. Rinse the inside with lots of cold water, making sure to remove any remaining innards, especially the plastic-like vertebra. Keep telling yourself this dish is really worth doing.

Now we deal with the head part. Make a cut just above the eyes to separate the tentacles. Discard the head and keep the tentacles.

To prepare the stuffing, combine breadcrumbs, parsley, chopped garlic and olive oil in a bowl. Season with salt and pepper and mix together well. Begin stuffing by spooning the mixture a bit at a time into the body of the squid, until it is ¾ full. Close the top with a cocktail toothpick.

Preheat oven to 400°F (200°C).

Season the squid with salt and pepper. Place a frying pan on high heat. Heat oil and add stuffed squid. Sear until they are brown on all sides. Place on a shallow roasting pan or casserole along with the tentacles, chopped tomato, white wine, parsley and a good shake of mild paprika. Bake for 30 minutes uncovered. Remove from oven and serve with steamed rice and lots of freshly squeezed lemon.

Chicken Nuggets / 92

Terracotta Baked Chicken Thighs with Sweet and Sour Tomato Sauce / 93

Raspberry Chicken with Ginger / 94

Roasted Stuffed Chicken Breast with Goat Cheese and Dill / 95

Grilled Chicken Breast and Coconut Curry / 96

Breast of Turkey with Leeks, Parsnips and Carrots / 97

Family Scramble / 98

Cheddar Cheese and Corn Soufflé / 99

Potato Omelet / 100

Poultry & Eggs

Chicken Nuggets

1¼ lb.	boneless and skinless chicken breast (about 3 halves)	625 g
1 cup	flour	250 mL
2 tsp.	salt	10 mL
½ tsp.	pepper	2 mL
2	eggs	2
½ cup	milk	125 mL
6 cups	cornflakes	1.5 L
4 Tbsp.	vegetable oil, divided	60 mL

YIELDS 16 TO 18 NUGGETS

You can make these homemade chicken nuggets ahead if you wish and then simply freeze them in self-sealing plastic bags. Our kids dip them in ketchup, and they seem to like them any time of day.

Preheat oven to 350°F (180°C).

Place chicken breasts between two sheets of plastic wrap and pound with a mallet to flatten to ½ inch (1.5 cm) thick. Cut them into nuggets about 1½ inches (4 cm) square. Crush cornflakes, or better still pulse in food processor, until they resemble fine breadcrumbs. Place seasoned flour in one bowl, lightly beaten eggs and milk in second bowl, and crushed cornflakes in third bowl. Dip each piece of chicken in the flour, then the egg, and finally coat with cornflake crumbs.

Rub the baking sheet with 2 Tbsp. (30 mL) oil. Place the nuggets on the baking sheet. Drizzle the remaining 2 Tbsp. (30 mL) of oil over them. Bake for 20 to 25 minutes. Turn the nuggets over halfway through the baking process.

Terracotta Baked Chicken Thighs with Sweet and Sour Tomato Sauce

🌿

This was one of the first recipes that Theresa cooked for me when we met. In those days she made it with chicken wings. I instantly loved the sweet and sour elements, which were somewhat new to me. It must be genetic because now it's one of our children's favourite dishes, especially served with basmati rice.

Preheat oven to 350°F (180°C).

Prepare Quick Tomato Sauce and allow to simmer while preparing chicken.

Heat vegetable oil in a heavy skillet on medium-high heat. Season chicken with salt and pepper. Coat well with flour and shake off excess. Place chicken in the hot oil and brown on both sides. Place thighs in an earthenware or Pyrex casserole dish.

Add sugar, red wine vinegar and cinnamon to tomato sauce. Mix well. Pour sweet-and-sour tomato sauce over the chicken thighs. Cover casserole dish with foil and bake for 30 minutes. Remove foil and continue to bake uncovered for another 30 minutes.

1 recipe	Quick Tomato Sauce (page 141)	1 recipe
¼ cup	vegetable oil	50 mL
8	chicken thighs	8
	salt and pepper	
½ cup	flour	125 mL
¼ cup	brown or white sugar	50 mL
¼ cup	red wine vinegar	50 mL
⅛ tsp.	cinnamon	0.5 mL

SERVES 4

Raspberry Chicken
with Ginger

❦

4	large free-range chicken breast halves	4
1 cup	mashed fresh raspberries	250 mL
2 Tbsp.	raspberry vinegar or red wine vinegar	30 mL
1 tsp.	grated ginger	5 mL
½ cup	Chardonnay	125 mL
	pepper	
1 tsp.	ground cumin	5 mL
2	sprigs fresh thyme	2
	salt	
1 cup	whipping cream	250 mL

SERVES 4

I developed this recipe in 1997, when we had a great crop of raspberries. The marinating process causes the chicken to turn a dark purplish colour which gives it a very exotic look and taste.

Place chicken in a bowl with raspberries, vinegar, ginger and Chardonnay. Season with pepper and cumin and thyme. (Season with salt just before cooking.) Cover and refrigerate overnight or at least 8 hours.

Preheat oven to 375°F (180°C).

Remove chicken from refrigerator and place in a heavy cast-iron skillet or roasting pan, along with the marinade. Season with salt and bake for 35 minutes or until cooked. Pour off any remaining juices into a saucepan.

Add cream to the pan juices and simmer over medium heat for about 5 minutes, or until thick enough to coat the back of a spoon. Check seasoning, strain and serve.

Roasted Stuffed Chicken Breast with Goat Cheese and Dill

❦

Stuffing under the skin is a really simple way to dress up a last-minute chicken dish. This is also great served cold as a picnic dish. All you need is a loaf of bread and a salad.

If you wish, you can change the type of herbs you use. Some other good flavours are tarragon, basil or chopped sweet red peppers. Try to find free-range chicken. There is a real difference in flavour and texture.

4 Tbsp.	goat cheese, or any low-fat cream cheese	60 mL
4 tsp.	finely chopped fresh dill	20 mL
4	large boneless chicken breast halves, with skin on	4
2 Tbsp.	vegetable oil	30 mL
½ tsp.	salt	2 mL
½ tsp.	freshly ground pepper	2 mL

SERVES 4

Preheat oven at 400°F (200°C).

Mix together the cheese and herbs in a small bowl.

Make a small opening for the cheese by simply loosening the skin away from the meat at the thick end of the breast to form a pocket. Fill a tablespoon (15 mL) with the cheese and herb mixture. Place the spoon under the skin and slide the mixture off the end by holding the skin down on the spoon. Press and spread the cheese evenly.

Drizzle the vegetable oil into a heavy roasting pan. Season the oil with salt and pepper. Dip the chicken breasts in the seasoned oil to coat completely. Roast, skin side up, for approximately 30 minutes.

Before serving, slice each breast diagonally in half. Baste with the pan juices.

Grilled Chicken Breast
and Coconut Curry

❦

CURRY SAUCE		
2 Tbsp.	butter	30 mL
½ cup	chopped onion	125 mL
2	cloves garlic, minced	2
1 Tbsp.	peeled and finely chopped fresh ginger	15 mL
½ cup	diced celery	125 mL
3 tsp.	curry powder	15 mL
½ tsp.	cumin	2 mL
3 tsp.	yellow mustard seeds	15 mL
14-oz. tin	coconut milk	398 mL
1 cup	chicken stock	250 mL
1	apple, peeled and diced	1
	juice of 1 orange	
2 Tbsp.	tomato paste	30 mL
2 Tbsp.	chopped cilantro	30 mL

GRILLED CHICKEN		
4	boneless chicken breast halves with skin on	4
1 Tbsp.	olive oil	15 mL
	salt & pepper	
½ tsp.	paprika	2 mL

SERVES 4

Adjusting the amount or type of curry powder can vary the heat of this dish. This recipe is a mild, fruity style. The sauce also works well with grilled seafood, such as prawns.

CURRY SAUCE: Melt butter over medium heat. Add onions and garlic. Cover and cook for 5 minutes. Then add ginger and celery and cook for a few more minutes. Add the curry powder, cumin and mustard seeds and cook for 2 to 3 minutes, uncovered. Add ⅔ tin coconut milk, stock, diced apple, orange juice and tomato paste. Reserve the remainder of the coconut milk for use in cooking basmati rice (page 40).

Reduce heat to low, stir all the ingredients together and simmer for 20 to 25 minutes. Before serving add the freshly chopped cilantro and season to taste.

GRILLED CHICKEN: Brush chicken breasts with oil. Season with salt, pepper and a shake of paprika. Broil or barbecue on medium-high heat for approximately 20 minutes until crispy skinned and cooked through.

To serve, make a mound of basmati rice (approximately 1 cup/250 mL) on each warmed plate. Place whole or sliced chicken on top of the rice. Pour curry sauce around the plate. Garnish with whole cilantro leaves.

FACING PAGE
Salmon on the Barbecue in Foil, page 76;
Grilled Asparagus with Sundried Tomato
Vinaigrette, page 12; New Potato Salad with
Buttermilk Dressing, page 35;
Grilled Chicken;
Shrimp and Pear Salad, page 36

Breast of Turkey with Leeks, Parsnips and Carrots

The beauty of this dish is that you can prepare the packets ahead of time. They will keep in the fridge for up to eight hours. The cooking is very hot and fast, just the way chefs cook in a restaurant, so it is important to have the turkey uniformly sliced. Serve with steamed rice or a potato dish.

Preheat oven to 500°F (260°C).

Tear off 4 pieces of aluminum foil, each about 11 x 12 inches (28 x 30 cm). Combine salt and pepper in a small bowl. Using half the mixture and dividing evenly, sprinkle a little salt and pepper into the centre of each foil sheet.

To escalope the turkey breast, cut the breast across into four ¾-inch (2 cm) slices.

Place 1 escalope of turkey breast on the salt and pepper on each sheet. Divide the julienned vegetables and spread evenly over the escalopes. Season each portion of turkey and vegetables evenly with remaining salt and pepper.

To make seasoned butter, combine butter with parsley, garlic, tarragon, salt and pepper. Dab each turkey breast with seasoned butter, then wrap up and seal the foil packets tightly.

Heat a heavy baking sheet in the oven for about 2 minutes, then arrange foil packets, folded side up, about 1 inch (2.5 cm) apart on the hot baking sheet. Bake for 8 minutes. Serve right away.

½ tsp.	coarse salt	2 mL
¾ tsp.	freshly ground black pepper	1.5 mL
1½-lb.	turkey breast, skinned and boned	750 g
1	medium leek, julienned (white part only)	1
1	medium carrot, julienned	1
1	medium parsnip, julienned	1
¼ cup	unsalted butter	50 mL
¼ cup	packed finely chopped Italian parsley	50 mL
½	small clove garlic, finely chopped	½
1 tsp.	chopped fresh tarragon	5 mL

SERVES 4

FACING PAGE
Dungeness Crab and Eggplant Cannelloni, page 87

Family Scramble

❧

2 Tbsp.	butter	30 mL
4 slices	bacon, cut in large dice	4 slices
1	small onion, finely chopped	1
4-6	medium button mushrooms, sliced	4-6
2	medium cooked potatoes, diced	2
6	eggs	6
3 Tbsp.	cheddar cheese, grated	45 mL
	salt and pepper	

SERVES 4

When we visit Mum in Britain she serves this, often accompanied by sausages and fried tomatoes. She has always made the best breakfasts.

Melt butter in a large nonstick frying pan. Add bacon, onion and mushrooms, and lightly sauté on medium high heat for a few minutes. Add cooked potatoes and stir until thoroughly heated through. Beat eggs and pour into pan, sprinkle with cheese and allow to cook slowly until the eggs set. Brown the top under a broiler if desired.

Cut into wedges and serve with crusty bread or toast.

Cheddar Cheese and Corn Soufflé

❦

Don't be intimidated by soufflé dishes. They're actually very easy to make. However, there is a saying about soufflés: "You wait for the soufflé. The soufflé does not wait for you." This is a centerpiece dish, and one that I hope will dazzle the kids into eating everything on their plates. I usually set the table with a heavy place mat or metal trivet in the centre and serve the soufflé in front of everybody.

Crispy bacon or grilled sausages are great with this. Sometimes I make Quick Tomato Sauce (page 141) as an accompaniment.

Preheat oven to 375°F (190°C).

Melt butter in a saucepan on medium heat. Mix flour into melted butter and cook gently until the mixture leaves the sides of the saucepan. Add the milk and stir continuously until mixture thickens. Remove from heat and stir in grated cheese and corn. Set aside and cool for 5 to 10 minutes. Meanwhile prepare the soufflé mould.

Coat the inside of a 2-qt. (2 L) soufflé dish with the softened butter. Sprinkle the Parmesan cheese into the dish. Rotate the dish so that the cheese coats the sides. Season with a few grindings of black pepper. Set aside.

Now separate the yolks from the whites of the eggs and add the yolks to the cooled sauce and mix in well. Place egg whites in a mixing bowl and whip up until they form stiff peaks. Gently fold half of the whipped egg whites into the sauce until all traces of the egg whites have disappeared. Carefully fold in remaining egg whites. Pour the mixture into the prepared soufflé dish. Place on the middle shelf of the oven and bake for approximately 35 minutes, until well risen. Serve immediately.

VARIATION: For a more substantial dish add well-cooked macaroni. Boil ½ cup (125 mL) macaroni in salted water for 20 minutes. Refresh under running water and drain very well. Add with the corn and cheese.

2 Tbsp.	butter	30 mL
2 Tbsp.	flour	30 mL
1 cup	milk	250 mL
1 cup	grated cheddar cheese	250 mL
½ cup	drained canned corn kernels	125 mL
6	eggs	6
1 Tbsp.	softened butter	15 mL
¼ cup	finely grated Parmesan cheese	50 mL
	freshly ground pepper	

SERVES 4

Potato Omelet

❦

⅓ cup	olive oil	75 mL
2	medium potatoes, peeled and thinly sliced	2
8	eggs	8
½ cup	milk	125 mL
½ tsp.	salt	2 mL
½ tsp.	pepper	2 mL
¼ cup	peas	50 mL

FRESH TOMATO SAUCE

1 Tbsp.	butter	15 mL
4	medium juicy ripe tomatoes, finely chopped	4
½ tsp.	sugar	2 mL
¼ tsp.	salt	1 mL
¼ tsp.	pepper	1 mL

SERVES 4

This is a variation of the famous Tortilla de España. It is very easy to prepare, and I always make this when we have guests at breakfast or brunch. It is very nice served with the Fresh Tomato Sauce, but is also delicious on its own, hot or cold. I like to spice it up with a little hot sauce.

Preheat oven to 400°F (200°C).

Place ovenproof 10-inch (25 cm) frying pan on medium-high heat. Add oil and sliced potatoes. Cover the pan and fry for 7 to 8 minutes, turning the potatoes occasionally. Meanwhile, whisk eggs, milk, salt and pepper in a bowl.

Remove the potatoes from the heat and pour the eggs over them. Sprinkle peas on top.

Place frying pan in oven and bake for 10 minutes uncovered. Meanwhile, make tomato sauce

When omelet is cooked, remove from oven and allow to cool for 5 minutes. Place a large platter on top of the pan and invert quickly to remove the omelet from the pan.

Cut omelet into pie-shaped wedges and serve as you would a cake. Serve the tomato sauce in a bowl or sauce boat.

FRESH TOMATO SAUCE: Place saucepan on medium-high heat. Melt butter and add tomatoes, sugar and salt and pepper. Cover and simmer on medium-low heat for 10 minutes.

VARIATIONS: Add finely chopped onion or peppers to the potatoes. Fresh herbs such as basil or thyme may also be added to the egg mixture.

Meat

Bistro Steaks

2 4-oz.	New York steaks	2 125 g
2 tsp.	mild Dijon mustard	10 mL
2 tsp.	vegetable oil	10 mL
2 Tbsp.	butter	25 mL
	juice of 1 lemon	

SERVES 2

SAUCE VARIATION

¼ cup	olive oil	50 mL
1	onion, sliced	1
1 Tbsp.	chopped garlic (2 cloves)	15 mL
¼ cup	coarsely chopped pitted black olives	50 mL
1	small bay leaf	1
2 cups	Quick Tomato Sauce (page 141)	500 mL
1 Tbsp.	chopped parsley	15 mL
	salt and pepper	

This steak dish is standard fare on most small café menus in France. The classic accompaniments are pommes frites and watercress salad, or mashed potatoes and French beans tossed with herbs and butter.

These steaks are at their best straight out of the pan and sizzling on warmed plates.

Trim off all the fat and any gristle from the steaks. Place each steak between two sheets of plastic wrap. Using the flat end of a meat tenderizer, pound out the steaks to double their original size, approximately ⅛ inch (3 mm) thick.

Combine mustard and oil and brush both sides of each steak with this mixture. Season with salt and a light sprinkle of ground pepper.

Heat a large nonstick or cast-iron frying pan on high heat. When hot, place the steaks in the pan and quickly sear for 1 to 2 minutes each side (no longer). Remove steaks from the pan straight onto warmed serving plates.

Now quickly make the sauce. Add butter and lemon juice to the pan and place back on the heat. As soon as the butter melts, stir and pour sauce over the steaks and serve.

VARIATION: *Tomato, Onion and Black Olive Sauce for Steaks*

This almost relish-like bistro sauce can be served hot or cold with seared meats such as lamb or beef. If you serve this with the steak you don't need the lemon-butter sauce.

In a heavy pan heat olive oil on medium-low heat. Sauté onion and garlic for 10 minutes, until tender and slightly browned. Add the olives, bay leaf and tomato sauce. Simmer on low heat for 20 minutes. Season with salt and freshly ground pepper and add chopped parsley.

Braised Veal Shanks with Tomato, Lemon and Parsley

🌿

I think this is the most popular family meat dish that we make. We always have steamed rice and lots of bread to mop up the sauce, and of course little spoons to scoop out the bone marrow. The secret is to buy really good quality small veal shanks and cook them slowly.

This is a great next-day dish too. Just reheat and serve.

Prepare tomato sauce.

Preheat oven to 325°F (160°C).

Season veal shanks and coat with flour. Heat a large frying pan and add oil. Fry veal shanks in shallow oil until light brown on all sides. Place in a baking dish approximately 9 x 13 inches (23 x 32.5 cm). Pour the tomato sauce over. Cover tightly with aluminum foil. Bake on low heat for 2 hours.

Combine lemon zest and parsley and sprinkle over shanks before serving.

1 recipe	Quick Tomato Sauce (page 141)	1 recipe
8	veal shanks, centre cut	8
	salt and pepper	
½ cup	flour	125 mL
2 Tbsp.	oil	30 mL
	grated zest of 1 lemon for garnish	
2 tsp.	chopped parsley	10 mL

SERVES 8

Roasted Pork Tenderloin
with Mushroom White Wine Sauce

❦

2 8-oz.	pork tenderloins	2 250 g
1 Tbsp.	vegetable oil	15 mL
	salt and pepper	
1 cup	sliced chanterelle or button mushrooms	250 mL
¼ cup	white wine	50 mL
¼ cup	unfiltered apple juice	50 mL
2 Tbsp.	mild Dijon mustard	25 mL
½ cup	whipping cream	125 mL

SERVES 4

Pork tenderloin is one of the most underestimated cuts of meat. There is virtually no waste. It's very tender and cooks very quickly. And it tastes delicious hot or cold.

Preheat oven to 375°F (190°C).

Brush tenderloins with the vegetable oil and season with salt and pepper. Preheat an unoiled heavy cast-iron pan or skillet on medium-high heat. Sear the tenderloins until brown on all sides. Place pan in oven and roast for approximately 10 to 15 minutes, until medium. Remove from the oven. Set pork tenderloins aside and keep warm.

Place the pan back on medium-high heat. Add the sliced mushrooms and cook for 5 minutes. Then pour the white wine and apple juice into the pan. Scrape the sides of the pan to pick up any of the roasting juices that remain. Blend in the mustard. Simmer until the liquid has reduced by about half. Add cream and season with salt and pepper to taste.

To serve, slice the tenderloin into neat little rounds. Drizzle sauce over top, and garnish with fresh sage leaves.

Sage Pork Chops
with Apple Compote

❦

These pork chops make a simple dinner. The bread coating keeps the chops moist and seems to tenderize them. The delicious apple compote can be made ahead and served hot or cold. It works well made with pears too.

Preheat oven to 375°F (190°C).

Season the chops with salt and pepper.

To make fresh breadcrumbs, simply pulse bread in a food processor for a few seconds. Then add the sage and pulse until the breadcrumbs are quite fine.

Oil a baking dish. Set up three bowls: one with the flour, one with the egg-and-milk mixture, and one with breadcrumbs. Dip the seasoned chops into the flour. Shake off excess flour, then dip chops in egg-milk mixture, and finally in the breadcrumb mixture. Pat well and place on oiled baking dish. Bake for 20 minutes. Turn the chops over and bake for a further 20 minutes. Serve with apple compote.

APPLE COMPOTE: Place all ingredients together in a heavy pot with a tight-fitting lid. Cook on low heat for 20 to 30 minutes. Remove from heat and serve hot or cold.

4-8	centre-cut pork chops	4-8
	salt and pepper	
1½ cups	fresh breadcrumbs	375 mL
1 Tbsp.	finely chopped fresh sage leaves	15 mL
1 Tbsp.	vegetable oil	15 mL
½ cup	flour	125 mL
1	egg, slightly beaten	1
¼ cup	milk	50 mL

APPLE COMPOTE

4	medium apples, peeled, cored and quartered (1¼ lbs./500 g)	4
½ cup	water	125 mL
2 Tbsp.	sugar	30 mL
1	small cinnamon stick (½ tsp./2 mL ground)	1

SERVES 4

Pork Side Ribs
and White Beans

❧

2 lbs.	pork side ribs	1 kg
2 cups	dry navy beans, washed and picked over	500 mL
8 cups	cold water	2 L
¼ cup	chopped celery	50 mL
1 cup	chopped carrots	250 mL
1 cup	chopped onion	250 mL
½ tsp.	ground cumin	2 mL
½ tsp.	ground coriander	2 mL
1	bay leaf	1
2	cloves garlic, chopped	2
1 Tbsp.	tomato paste	15 mL
2 tsp.	salt and pepper	10 mL
1 Tbsp.	chopped cilantro leaves	15 mL
	sprigs of cilantro for garnish	

RIB SAUCE		
1 Tbsp.	honey	15 mL
1 cup	barbecue sauce	250 mL

SERVES 6

Here's a comforting winter dish that's great for after hiking or skiing. The first part can be made ahead of time, then all you have to do is bake the ribs and your dinner is ready.

Use your favourite homemade or commercial barbecue sauce, or try the sauce on page 109 (which doesn't require the extra honey).

Place all of the ingredients except cilantro in a large soup pot and bring to a simmer on medium heat. Skim off any foam that surfaces as it simmers. Turn down the heat to low, cover and cook for 1 hour. Remove from the heat and take out the ribs. Check the seasoning on the beans. (These beans like lots of salt.) Set aside.

RIB SAUCE: Line a baking sheet with aluminum foil.

Cut ribs into 4-rib segments and place on the sheet. Combine honey and barbecue sauce in a bowl. Brush the ribs with the sauce, and bake at 350°F (180°C) for 15 minutes. Turn the ribs over and brush again with more sauce. Bake for a further 15 minutes.

To serve, heat the beans and add the cilantro at the last minute. Ladle out onto warm soup plates. Top with the baked ribs. Garnish with sprigs of cilantro.

Baked Spiced Ham

❦

Several of the recipes in this book are family favourites that we serve time and time again throughout the year. We especially enjoy this one during the Christmas holidays, with lovely winter vegetables like brussels sprouts and red cabbage. Traditionally we like to serve it with a big dollop of parsley sauce on the side.

Cold baked ham makes great leftovers.

Preheat oven to 325°F (160°C).

Score the ham in a crisscross pattern. Brush on the marmalade, and stud the ham all over with whole cloves. Dust with cinnamon. Pour cider or juice into roasting pan around the ham and bake for 1½ to 2 hours until golden brown and glazed. Midway through the cooking process, baste with pan juices.

PARSELY SAUCE: Melt butter in heavy saucepan on medium heat. Add the flour and cook gently, stirring constantly until the flour is well incorporated.

Remove the butter and flour mixture from heat and pour in the milk and parsley. Return the pan to medium heat and bring the sauce to a simmer, stirring constantly with a whisk or wooden spoon for 5 minutes or until thickened. Season to taste with salt and pepper.

9 lb.	ham on the bone (cooked)	4 kg
½ cup	marmalade or apricot preserves	125 mL
2 Tbsp.	cloves (30 cloves)	30 mL
1 tsp.	ground cinnamon	5 mL
1½ cups	apple cider or juice	375 mL

PARSLEY SAUCE		
2 Tbsp.	butter	30 mL
2 Tbsp.	unbleached flour	30 mL
2 cups	milk	500 mL
2 Tbsp.	chopped fresh parsley	30 mL
	salt and pepper	

SERVES 8 TO 10

Marinated Ostrich Filet
with Vermouth and Rosemary

MARINADE		
1 cup	vegetable oil	250 mL
2 Tbsp.	mustard seeds	30 mL
2 Tbsp.	fennel seeds	30 mL
2 Tbsp.	coriander seeds	30 mL
2 lbs.	ostrich fan filet or back tenderloin	1 kg

SAUCE		
2 Tbsp.	butter	30 mL
½ cup	finely chopped shallots	125 mL
2 tsp.	minced garlic	10 mL
¼ cup	red wine vinegar	50 mL
½ cup	red vermouth	125 mL
1 tsp.	chopped fresh rosemary leaves	2 mL
2 cups	beef demi-glace, or beef stock reduced until it coats the back of a spoon	500 mL

SERVES 4

This dish is very popular at the restaurant, and I felt we should include it here because we're beginning to see ostrich appearing in stores. It is a lovely lean meat with a flavour like the best beef. The fan filet corresponds to the succulent "oyster" on a turkey.

MARINADE: Combine oil and spices in non-reactive container. Cut ostrich into 4 equal pieces and place in marinade. Refrigerate overnight, covered.

SAUCE: Melt the butter in a saucepan, then sauté the shallots and garlic until tender. Add the vinegar and reduce until almost gone. Add the vermouth and rosemary, then reduce by half. Add the demi-glace and simmer for 30 minutes. Strain.

This sauce can be made a day in advance and will actually taste better after the flavour has developed for a day. Refrigerate until needed and reheat before serving.

Remove ostrich from marinade and season with salt and pepper. Grill on high heat, or pan roast at 400°F (200°C) until medium rare, about 5 minutes on each side. Remove to a warm place and rest for 3 to 5 minutes. Slice across the grain and serve with sauce.

Spareribs for Kids

❦

Baby back ribs have way less fat than the side ribs. They are more expensive, but once in a while I like to get them because they're a real treat for the kids. Don't worry about the sauce being too spicy, as any hot flavours soften with cooking.

Preheat oven to 400°F (200°C).

Trim any fat from the ribs. Cut into portions, approximately 8 ribs per serving.

Combine all other ingredients in a bowl for barbecue sauce.

Line a baking sheet with aluminum foil. Place the ribs on the baking sheet and brush both sides liberally with barbecue sauce. Place in the oven and bake for 10 minutes. Turn the ribs over, brush with a little more sauce and bake for a further 10 minutes. Turn over and brush with more sauce. Set oven to broil. Leave rack at middle of oven. Broil for 5 minutes until brown and crispy. (If your broiler is too small to keep the ribs well removed from the heat, just continue baking for the same amount of time.)

3 lbs.	pork back ribs	1.5 kg
1 cup	ketchup	250 mL
3 Tbsp.	Worcestershire sauce	45 mL
¼ cup	cider vinegar	50 mL
1	clove garlic, crushed	1
2 Tbsp.	mild Dijon mustard	30 mL
4 Tbsp.	liquid honey	60 mL
½ tsp.	salt	2 mL
½ tsp.	Tabasco sauce (optional)	2 mL

SERVES 4

Roasted Rack of Lamb
with Minted Celery Root

2 racks	fresh lamb	2
2	carrots, large dice	2
1	onion, quartered	1
1	stalk celery, coarsely chopped	1
1 Tbsp.	flour	15 mL
½ cup	red wine or water	125 mL
1 Tbsp.	liquid honey	15 mL
1 Tbsp.	mild Dijon mustard	15 mL
	pinch ground cumin	
	salt and freshly ground pepper	
1 sprig	rosemary	1 sprig
1	bay leaf, crushed	1
1 cup	red wine	250 mL
1 Tbsp.	fresh mint, chopped	15 mL
2 cups	matchstick-cut celery root	500 mL

SERVES 4

Sometimes I like to pull out the stops and spend a good part of the day puttering in the kitchen. This is a dish for those days.

If you're not sure how or don't wish to clean the lamb yourself, ask the butcher. Remember to keep the trimmings for stock.

Celery root should be firm and heavy for its size. Be aware that there's quite a bit of waste, as you cut off the gnarled outside bits. The inside should go into acidulated water as soon as it's cut so it won't go brown.

Preheat oven at 400°F (200°C).

Clean and trim the fat cap from the racks of lamb. This includes some meat. Trim out the meat between the end bones. Coarsely chop all of the trimmings and place them in a heavy roasting pan or skillet along with the carrots, onion and celery. Place the pan or skillet in the oven and roast until brown, turning occasionally. This should take about 45 minutes.

When browned, transfer meat trimmings to a saucepan, leaving any fat in the roasting pan. Mix the flour into the fat. Rinse the roasting pan out with the cold water or red wine, and add to saucepan. Now cover with more cold water and bring to boil on medium-high heat. Turn down the heat to low and then simmer for 1 hour. This mini stock will serve as a base for the minted celery root sauce.

Combine honey and mustard and rub the racks of lamb with the mixture. Season with cumin, salt and pepper. Place in a nonreactive dish. Sprinkle with rosemary leaves and crushed bay leaf. Pour the wine over the lamb. Cover and allow to marinate in the refrigerator for 2 to 3 hours or longer.

To roast the lamb, preheat the oven to 400°F (200°C).

Remove the lamb from the marinade and pat dry with a paper towel. Reserve marinade and set aside. Place a heavy ovenproof skillet on medium-high heat. Rub the lamb with a small amount of vegetable oil. Place the racks in the pan and brown on both sides. After browning, put pan into the preheated oven with meat side down and roast approximately 15 to 20 minutes. Remove meat from the pan and place on a warmed platter. Turn down oven to lowest setting. When oven temperature has lowered, place lamb back in to keep warm. This will allow the rare meat to rest and become pink.

Swish out the roasting pan with the marinade, making sure to pick up any residue that sticks to the bottom of the pan. This really adds to the flavour of the sauce. Add this to the stock that has been simmering. Check for taste and season with a small amount of salt and freshly ground pepper. Simmer for approximately 15 minutes. Strain into another pot and add the chopped mint leaves and celery root sticks. Simmer for another 10 minutes until celery root is tender.

To serve, divide lamb racks into chops and lightly coat each chop with a ladle of sauce and the celery root.

The lamb can be served with a selection of vegetable purées, and a green vegetable such as brussels sprout leaves or green beans.

Roast Lamb Loin

2	whole lamb loins (approx. 1 lb/500 g)	2
1 Tbsp.	Dijon mustard	15 mL
½ tsp.	ground cumin	2 mL
½ tsp.	salt	2 mL
1 tsp.	cracked pepper	5 mL

SERVES 4 TO 6

This lamb loin goes well with Honey-Glazed Carrots (page 49) because the lamb itself does not have a sauce. The carrots not only add sweetness, but also act as a sauce. For starch I recommend the Potato Dumplings with Basil on page 43.

Restaurant chefs, when they are roasting small prime cuts of meat, always use pans that are made with metal handles, so they can go from stovetop directly into the oven. This enables the chef to cook the meat very quickly without having to transfer the meat from a hot pan into a cold one.

Clean lamb loins and trim them of all fat. Mix together mustard, cumin, salt and pepper in a bowl. Rub the lamb loins with the mixture. Set aside.

Preheat oven to 450°F (200°C).

Place the lamb loins in a heavy dry pan and sear on all sides until browned. Place lamb in a preheated shallow roasting pan. Roast for 7 to 10 minutes for medium rare (longer if preferred).

Remove from oven and keep warm for 10 minutes prior to serving to let the meat rest. Carve into thin slices and serve on warm plates. A nice garnish for your plates would be a sprig of basil or watercress.

Breads

Cheese Straws

❧

	flour	
7 oz.	puff pastry (½ block)	200 g
½ cup	Parmesan or cheddar cheese, grated medium-fine	125 mL
¼ tsp.	cayenne (optional)	1 mL

YIELDS 20 PIECES

These are really good with soups. Children love them as snacks and they make a good addition to a school lunch.

Preheat oven to 400°F (200°C).

Roll pastry on floured board to a 9 x 12-inch (23 x 30 cm) rectangle. Scatter on the grated cheese, and if you like, a good shake or two of hot cayenne. Fold over one side of the pastry to cover the cheese, then roll out again. This will blend the cheese and spice right into the pastry.

Using a pizza cutter or sharp knife, cut pastry into ½ x 9-inch strips (1.5 x 23 cm). Line a baking sheet with parchment paper and lay on the strips, twisting them into a corkscrew pattern as you lay them out.

Bake for 12 to 15 minutes.

Parmesan Crisps

You'll find these invaluable. Nothing could be easier to make, but nothing could taste better. They're a great accompaniment to soups or salads, and an interesting addition to a bread basket. Try making them into festive shapes such as hearts for Valentine's Day or bells for Christmas. They should be stored covered in a cool dry place.

Preheat oven to 375°F (190°C).

Line a baking or cookie sheet with parchment paper.

Sprinkle 1 heaping Tbsp. (15 mL) grated cheese onto the baking sheet and form a 1½ x 5-inch rectangle (4 x 12.5 cm). Repeat until all the cheese is used. Bake for 5 minutes until golden brown. Cool and serve.

| ½ cup | coarsely grated Parmesan | 125 mL |

YIELDS 6

Big Dippers

1	long thin baguette	1
3 tsp.	olive oil	15 mL
3 tsp.	butter, melted	15 mL
½ cup	grated Parmesan cheese	125 mL

YIELDS 6 DIPPERS

These are great with steamed clams, soup or salad. I like to cut them really long and thin so they work the same as breadsticks.

Preheat oven to 350°F (180°C).

Slice the baguette at a very oblique angle to obtain 6 ¼-inch-thick slices that are about 9 inches long (5 mm x 23 cm). Place slices of bread on a baking sheet. Mix together butter and olive oil. Brush each slice of bread with 1 tsp. (5 mL) of the mixture. Sprinkle the cheese evenly over top. Bake for 8 to 10 minutes, until cheese is melted and bread is crisp.

If you like you can add chopped fresh tomatoes and sprinkle with chopped fresh basil.

Parmesan Profiteroles

We put these in the bread baskets at the restaurant and people beg for more. Hot out of the oven, they are irresistible, and consequently this is our most-requested recipe.

Profiteroles are surprisingly simple to prepare. They also make wonderful hors d'oeuvres when they're cooled, sliced open and filled with such things as smoked salmon and dilled cream cheese, or tuna tartare—much more sophisticated than just plain crackers.

Preheat oven to 425°F (220°C).

In a saucepan, stir together the butter, milk, water and salt. Bring to a simmer slowly over medium heat. Reduce heat to low. Add the flour quickly to the liquid and, using a wooden spoon, mix to form a ball. Mix for about 30 to 40 seconds until a dry ball is formed.

Place dough in electric mixer with a paddle attachment, or mix by hand with a large wooden spoon. Mix on low speed while adding one egg at a time to the dough. Make sure each egg has been absorbed before adding another. Add the grated cheese and season with pepper.

Place a round piping tip into a pastry bag and fill bag with mixture. Pipe out 24 small profiteroles, about 1-inch (2.5 cm) in diameter, onto baking sheet lined with parchment paper. (You can make them larger if you wish.) Pat down any peaks with your fingertip. Place in oven and bake for 10 to 15 minutes until golden brown. Open the oven door a crack and bake for 10 more minutes.

6 Tbsp.	butter	90 mL
⅔ cup	milk	150 mL
½ cup	water	125 mL
1 tsp.	salt	5 mL
1⅓ cups	flour	325 mL
3	eggs	3
⅓ cup	finely grated Parmesan cheese	75 mL
	cracked black pepper or cayenne	

YIELDS 2 DOZEN

Green Olive Focaccia

❧

1 Tbsp.	yeast	15 mL
1 tsp.	sugar	5 mL
1½ cups	warm water	375 mL
3½-4½ cups	flour	560-720 g
½ cup	chopped green olives	125 mL
½ cup	olive oil	125 mL
1 tsp.	salt	5 mL
	rock salt	

YIELDS 2 ROUNDS

MEDITERRANEAN GRILLED FOCACCIA SANDWICH

2	focaccia rounds or sourdough baguette	2
16-20	Roasted Roma Tomato slices (page 145) or 4 raw tomatoes, sliced	16-20
3	bocconcini, sliced	3
12	fresh basil leaves	12

Breadmaking is therapy. Handmade bread is the workout you didn't have this morning. It is a labour of love, but well worth the effort. I've taught my son, David, how to work with yeast breads, and he's most intrigued.

Combine yeast, sugar and warm water in a large bowl and let sit for 10 minutes until it becomes frothy and creamy coloured. Add flour, green olives, olive oil and salt and mix together. Turn dough out onto a floured surface and knead for 5 to 7 minutes until dough is smooth and glossy.

Place in an oiled bowl and cover with a cloth. Let the dough proof in a warm place for 1 hour, or until it has doubled in volume. Punch down and let it proof again for 35 minutes. The dough may be shaped into individual rounds or rolled into a rectangle. Brush a baking sheet with a bit of olive oil and sprinkle with cornmeal. Place the shaped dough on the baking sheet, and let the dough rise until it doubles in volume—approximately 30 minutes. Prick dough all over using a fork. Brush generously with olive oil and sprinkle with rock salt.

Preheat oven to 350°F (180°C).

Bake for 20 to 25 minutes, depending on the size of the loaf. When it's done the loaf will sound hollow when the bottom is tapped.

MEDITERRANEAN GRILLED FOCACCIA SANDWICH: Once focaccia is cooled, slice each one in half crosswise. Brush each side with olive oil. Fill 2 of the halves with alternating layers of tomato, bocconcini and basil. Put remaining 2 halves on top and press down. Then place on barbecue or in cast-iron frying pan over low heat. Grill for 10 minutes on each side.

Breadsticks

I have a soft spot for breadsticks. Not only are they great eating, but visually they are very appealing as a centerpiece on the table.

Roll dough out into a 12-inch square (30 cm). Cut into strips ¾ inch (2 cm) wide. Place on a baking sheet that has been sprinkled with cornmeal. Let breadsticks rise for 15 minutes. Brush with olive oil and sprinkle with coarse salt, poppy seeds or rosemary. Bake at 375°F (190°C) for 15 minutes.

1 recipe	pizza dough (page 120)	1 recipe
	cornmeal	
	olive oil	
1-2 Tbsp.	rock salt or poppy seeds or chopped rosemary	15-30 mL

YIELDS 15

Green Onion Pizza Cakes

PIZZA DOUGH		
1 tsp.	yeast	5 mL
1½ tsp.	sugar	7 mL
1 cup	warm water	250 mL
2½ cups	flour	625 mL
2 Tbsp.	oil	30 mL
1½ tsp.	salt	7 mL
⅔ cup	chopped green onions (about 4)	150 mL
	vegetable oil for frying	

YIELDS 20 TO 25 CAKES

These are incredibly delicious and versatile. Serve them warm with soup or salad. Or top them with smoked salmon, prosciutto or cheese for hors d'oeuvres. For a more spicy variation, add chopped anchovies, sundried tomatoes and black Niçoise olives.

For this recipe you can make your own pizza dough, purchase it ready-made from a bakery or use the frozen bread dough available at supermarkets.

PIZZA DOUGH: Place the yeast, sugar and warm water in a bowl and let the yeast bubble and froth. This will take about 10 minutes. Add the flour, oil and salt and stir together. Turn out onto a floured surface and knead for 5 to 7 minutes. Place dough in an oiled bowl and cover with plastic wrap. Let rise in a warm place until it has doubled in volume. This will take about an hour. Punch the dough down and allow to double in volume again. This will take about ½ hour.

Roll dough out to form a 12-inch (30 cm) square. Scatter green onions evenly across the surface. Roll up tightly as you would for a jelly roll. Slice into ¼-inch rounds (5 mm). Flatten with your hands to half the thickness.

Fry in a lightly oiled nonstick pan on medium-low heat for 8 to 10 minutes per side, until golden brown and cooked through.

Scones

I grew up with the tradition of afternoon tea. The tea always included freshly baked scones, homemade jam and clotted Devon cream. If you can't find Devon cream you can always serve them with whipped cream.

I like to use the almond-flavoured variation as the basis for individual strawberry shortcakes.

1¼ cups	flour	300 mL
¼ tsp.	salt	1 mL
2 tsp.	baking powder	10 mL
4 Tbsp.	butter, cut into chunks	60 mL
4 Tbsp.	sultana raisins, optional	60 mL
½ cup	milk	125 mL
	milk to glaze	

YIELDS 8

Preheat oven to 400°F (200°C).

Sift flour, salt and baking powder together in a bowl. Add butter and rub it in with your fingers until mixture resembles fine breadcrumbs. Stir in sultanas.

Make a well in centre of mixture and pour in milk. Mix lightly with a spoon until a soft dough is formed.

Turn dough onto a floured board and knead gently until smooth. Roll out dough to ½-inch thickness (1.5 cm) and cut into rounds with a 2-inch cookie cutter (5 cm).

Place scones on a lightly greased baking sheet and brush tops with milk. Bake for 10 minutes or until scones are well risen and golden. Remove from oven and cool on wire rack.

VARIATION: *Almond Scones*

Substitute 2 Tbsp. (30 mL) ground almonds for 2 Tbsp. (30 mL) of the flour, and add a few drops of almond essence. Omit the rasins.

Welsh Cakes

1¼ cups	flour	300 mL
1 tsp.	baking powder	5 mL
¼ tsp.	salt	1 mL
½ tsp.	freshly grated nutmeg	2 mL
½ cup	butter	125 mL
½ cup	white sugar	125 mL
¼ cup	currants	50 mL
1	egg, lightly beaten	1
1-2 Tbsp.	milk	15-30 mL

YIELDS 16

This is a family recipe that my mother still makes. These rarely last long in our house, but if there are any left over, they make a great lunchbox snack. You can dust them with sifted icing sugar.

Sift together the flour, baking powder, salt and nutmeg. Rub in the butter until the mixture resembles fine breadcrumbs. Add sugar and currants and stir in beaten egg. Mix to form a stiff dough, adding a very little milk if necessary. Gather up dough and form a ball. Place on floured surface and roll out to ¼-inch thickness (5 mm). Cut out with 2-inch (5 cm) cookie cutter.

Lightly oil and preheat a griddle or nonstick frying pan on medium heat. When hot, test with a little dough. If griddle is too hot it will burn, and if not hot enough will not brown. Cook cakes for 5 minutes or until evenly browned. Turn over and cook for a further 5 minutes. Between batches wipe griddle with an oiled paper towel. Serve warm or cold.

Desserts

Bourbon Chocolate Cake

7 oz.	semisweet chocolate	200 g
1¼ cups	boiling water	300 mL
1 tsp.	baking soda	5 mL
¼ cup	bourbon	50 mL
½ cup	unsalted butter, soft	125 mL
¼ cup	white sugar	50 mL
½ cup	brown sugar	125 mL
1	egg	1
1½ cups	flour	375 mL
½ tsp.	salt	2 mL
¾ tsp.	baking powder	4 mL
1 Tbsp.	cocoa powder	15 mL

SWEETENED
WHIPPED CREAM

1 cup	whipping cream	250 mL
2 Tbsp.	sugar	30 mL
½ tsp.	vanilla	2 mL

SERVES 10

This is a very rich, moist chocolate cake that has the wonderful flavour of bourbon coming through.

Preheat oven to 350°F (180°C).

Line the bottom of a 10-inch (3L) springform pan with parchment paper. Butter and flour the pan. The parchment paper makes it easier to remove the cake from the pan after it is baked.

Place chocolate in a bowl and pour boiling water over top. Stir until chocolate is melted. Add soda and stir to dissolve. Then add bourbon and set aside.

In a large bowl, beat butter until smooth. Add white and brown sugar and beat until well blended. Add egg and continue to beat until egg is incorporated into the butter mixture.

In another bowl, sift together all the dry ingredients. Add dry ingredients and warm chocolate mixture alternately to batter, beginning and ending with dry ingredients, beating between each addition. Pour batter into prepared pan.

Bake 40 to 50 minutes, or until the edges have pulled away from the sides of the pan. Cool 10 to 15 minutes before removing cake from pan.

To serve, dust each slice with icing sugar. Serve with a dollop of sweetened vanilla whipped cream over the side of each portion.

SWEETENED WHIPPED CREAM: In a chilled bowl, whip the cream until it holds its shape. Add the sugar and vanilla and beat for a few seconds longer to combine. Chilling the bowl helps speed up the whipping process.

Grape Clafoutis

❧

This very easy country-French baked custard takes only a few minutes to prepare, and can be baking in the oven while you are having dinner.

You can also substitute fresh pitted cherries or small pitted plums for the grapes. You may have to cook it longer because they alter the moisture content.

Remove grapes from stems, wash and drain well.

Preheat oven to 400°F (200°C).

Sift flour into a large bowl with the salt. Add sugar and blend in the eggs, adding one at a time. Mix thoroughly. Gradually add the cold milk.

Butter a 10-inch (3L) ovenproof dish and arrange the grapes on the base. Cover with batter. Bake for 40 minutes. Remove from oven.

When it's cooled slightly you can glaze the clafoutis with the red currant jelly or simply sprinkle 2 to 3 Tbsp. (30-45 mL) white sugar on top. To glaze with jelly, melt the jelly over low heat. Spread over top the clafoutis. Serve hot or warm.

1½ lbs.	red seedless grapes	750 g
¾ cup	flour	175 mL
	pinch salt	
¾ cup	sugar	175 mL
4	eggs	4
3 cups	cold milk	750 mL
2 Tbsp.	butter	30 mL
½ cup	red currant jelly for glaze	125 mL

SERVES 6

Green Apple Tarte Tatin

❦

PASTRY		
1½ cups	flour	375 mL
½ cup	cornmeal	125 mL
1 Tbsp.	sugar	15 mL
1 tsp.	salt	5 mL
½ cup	butter	125 mL
¼ cup	cold water	50 mL

FILLING		
1 cup	sugar	250 mL
¼ cup	butter	50 mL
¼ cup	water	50 mL
6	green apples	6

SERVES 6

When I prepared this classic French dessert for the photo in the book even my pastry chef, Carolyn, was impressed. I like to make this with green apples because their high pectin content gives a jellylike texture to the caramel, but it can also be made with fresh pears or peaches.

You will find as you practise making this dessert that you can vary the intensity and the colour of the caramel by cooking the sugar and butter more or less.

PASTRY: Prepare the pastry by combining flour, cornmeal, sugar and salt in a large bowl. Cut butter into small pieces and rub into flour mixture until mealy. Add water and stir until just combined. Cover and allow to rest in the fridge for 20 minutes.

FILLING: Preheat oven to 400°F (200°C).

In a 10-inch (25 cm) cast-iron or heavy ovenproof pan, combine sugar, butter and water.

Stir and place on medium-high heat. Boil the mixture gently. You don't need to stir, but watch it carefully. When it turns amber, remove from heat. Have a large bowl of ice water ready. Place the hot pan on top of the ice water in order to stop the browning process immediately.

Peel, core and quarter apples. Arrange the quartered apples in a circular pattern on top of the caramelized sugar, completely filling the bottom of the pan.

Now roll out the pastry on a floured board and cut to fit inside the top of the pan. A plate makes a good guide. Place pastry over the apples. Do not cut vents in pastry.

Bake for 20 to 25 minutes until pastry is golden and cooked through. Allow to cool for 15 to 20 minutes. Run a knife around the edge and carefully invert onto a serving platter that has a rim. This is done by holding the platter on top of the pan and flipping it over quickly.

Serve it with vanilla ice cream or unsweetened whipped cream.

Sherry Trifle

🌿

½ lb.	sponge cake	250 g
4 Tbsp.	raspberry jam	60 mL
¾ cup	sherry	175 mL
	CUSTARD	
3 cups	milk	750 mL
⅔ cup	sugar	150 mL
4 Tbsp.	cornstarch	60 mL
2 tsp.	vanilla	10 mL
3	egg yolks	3
1½ cups	whipping cream	375 mL
2 Tbsp.	icing sugar	30 mL
12	maraschino cherries	12
	mint sprigs	
¼ cup	toasted almond slivers	50 mL

SERVES 6 TO 8

Trifle is the quintessential British dessert—a wonderful example of what can happen when you combine humble ingredients. In Wales the cut-glass bowl of trifle is a feature of every Christmas dinner or buffet.

For adults, the addition of a good sherry is a must. For a kids-only party, simply substitute fruit juice and some soft fruit, such as strawberries.

Halve sponge cake crosswise; spread one layer with jam. Place second layer on top of jam like a sandwich. Cut into large pieces, 1½ inches (4 cm) square. Place squares of cake in trifle dish. Pour sherry over cake and set aside.

To make the custard, scald 2½ cups (625 mL) of the milk in a medium saucepan. In another medium saucepan, mix together the remaining ½ cup (125 mL) cold milk, sugar and cornstarch. Pour the hot milk into this mixture. Place over medium-low heat, stirring constantly until liquid thickens and begins to bubble a little. This will take about 5 to 7 minutes. In a bowl, whisk together egg yolks and vanilla. Slowly add a little of the hot milk mixture to the yolks, stirring continuously. Pour mixture back into the saucepan, stir together and cook over low heat for 1 minute.

Remove from stovetop and pour custard over the cake in the trifle dish. Cool and then cover with plastic wrap and let sit in fridge overnight. This allows the sherry flavours to permeate. Top the trifle with sweetened whipped cream and garnish with cherries, mint and toasted almonds.

FACING PAGE
Salmon Terrine, page 16;
Pommes Anna, page 46; Baked Sweet Onions
Gratinée, page 54;
Baked Fanny Bay Oysters, page 89;
Sherry Trifle

Baked Stuffed Apples

❧

This is a good way to make stuffed apples because the foil keeps all the juices in. They can even be cooked on a barbecue or campfire this way.

Preheat oven to 350°F (180°C).

Wash and core the apples.

In small bowl, mix together the raisins, butter, brown sugar and cinnamon. Then place each apple on a 10-inch (25 cm) square of foil and stuff with the mixture. Seal up and place on a baking sheet. Bake for 45 to 60 minutes. To check for doneness, pierce the top of the apple through the foil with the point of a knife. Remove from the oven.

When slightly cool, carefully remove each apple from the foil. Set on a plate, along with a scoop of vanilla ice cream. Pour the cooking juices over top of the ice cream and garnish with a sprig of fresh mint.

4	large green cooking apples	4
4 Tbsp.	raisins	60 mL
4 Tbsp.	brown sugar	60 mL
4 Tbsp.	butter	60 mL
1 tsp.	ground cinnamon	5 mL

SERVES 4

FACING PAGE
Green Apple Tarte Tatin, page 126

Poached Pears with Ginger and White Wine

6	pears	6
2 cups	fruity white wine such as Gewurztraminer or Riesling	500 mL
2 cups	cold water	500 mL
¾ cup	sugar	175 mL
½ cup	roughly sliced ginger root, not peeled	125 mL
2	vanilla pods or 2 tsp. (10 mL) of vanilla extract	2

SERVES 6

This fruit dish makes a great holiday dessert. The ginger is very intense because you let the pears absorb the flavour for two to three days. Serve with vanilla bean ice cream.

Any leftover syrup can be used to make a refreshing beverage. Combine 2 ounces of syrup with 8 ounces of soda water and a twist of lemon

Peel the ripe pears and remove ¾ of the length of the core: starting at the bottom, first use an apple corer, then remove the core with a peeler. Keep the stem intact.

Place the pears in a medium-sized pot. Cover with the wine, water and sugar, and then add the ginger root and vanilla pods. Bring to a boil, then cover and simmer on low heat until the fruit is tender when pricked with a knife. Set aside to cool, then refrigerate for 2 to 3 days.

Blueberry Tart

❦

This is the dessert we served to Presidents Clinton and Yeltsin at the summit dinner in 1993. President Clinton had requested blueberries and we had to fly them in specially from the White House mess because they were out of season here. The night before the official dinner, all of the menu items had to be prepared and tasted by the White house and military tasting panel

PASTRY: Preheat oven to 350°F (180°C).

Combine flour, butter and icing sugar in a food processor until it forms a ball. Press and pat into a 10-inch (25 cm) tart pan with removable bottom. Prick bottom with a fork, line with parchment paper and pie beans. Bake for 20 minutes. Allow crust to cool before adding filling.

FILLING: Mix the sugar, cornstarch, lemon peel and cinnamon together. Set aside. Into a large saucepan, pour 1 cup (250 mL) of the blueberries and the water and bring to a boil. Add the sugar mixture and lemon juice. Cook until thickened, stirring constantly, about 3 to 4 minutes. Cool. Add the remaining 5 cups (1.25 L) of berries to the mixture. Spoon into prebaked and cooled pastry shell.

PASTRY		
1½ cups	white flour, sifted	375 mL
¾ cup	unsalted butter, room temperature, not soft	175 g
⅓ cup	icing sugar	75 mL

FILLING		
¾ cup	sugar	175 mL
4 Tbsp.	cornstarch	65 mL
1 tsp.	lemon zest	5 mL
¼ tsp.	ground cinnamon	2 mL
6 cups	fresh blueberries	1.5 L
2 cups	cold water	500 mL
2 Tbsp.	fresh lemon juice	30 mL

SERVES 6 TO 8

Country-Style
Fruit Custard Tart

❦

PASTRY		
1½ cups	white flour, sifted	240 g
¾ cup	unsalted butter, room temperature, not soft	175 g
⅓ cup	icing sugar	75 mL

PEAR FILLING		
½ cup	ground almonds	125 mL
1½ lbs.	Bartlett pears (4-5), peeled and cored	750 g
2 Tbsp.	white sugar	30 mL
⅛ tsp.	cinnamon	0.5 mL

CUSTARD		
2	eggs	2
1 cup	light cream	250 mL
¼ cup	sugar	50 mL

SERVES 8

I am not the world's biggest dessert fan, although I have been known to consume a Belgian chocolate or two. However, I really do enjoy desserts made with fruit. Theresa makes two variations of this custard tart, both family favourites.

For the pear, choose firm but ripe Bartlett pears. For the rhubarb, choose bright-coloured stalks.

PASTRY: Combine flour, butter and icing sugar in a food processor until it forms a ball. Trace the bottom of 10-inch springform pan onto parchment paper. Cut out the circle and place it in the pan. This will make it easier to remove the tart onto a serving plate after it is baked. Use approximately ⅔ of the dough to line the bottom of the pan, and press the remainder up the sides. It works well to form it into a roll first, and then press it evenly up the sides (about 1 inch/2.5 cm). Place in fridge while you cut up fruit.

PEAR FILLING: Scatter ground almonds on bottom of chilled pie shell.

Slice pears in eighths. Arrange the pear slices in a slightly overlapping circular pattern. Sprinkle pears with sugar and cinnamon. Bake at 375°F (190°C) for 20 minutes.

CUSTARD: Beat together eggs, cream and sugar. Remove partially baked tart from oven and pour custard on top. Return to oven and bake until custard is set, crust is lightly browned, and pears are tender, about 25 to 30 minutes.

Cool tart on a rack completely before removing from pan. May be served warm or at room temperature. Garnish with sweetened whipped cream.

VARIATION: This tart is also delicious using rhubarb. For the filling use 3 cups (750 mL) of cut-up rhubarb and ¼ cup (50 mL) sugar. Omit the ground almonds and cinnamon. Increase the sugar to ¾ cup (175 mL) in the custard. The baking time stays the same.

Vanilla Cream Pudding

This is one of Theresa's quick dessert solutions, which she inherited from her mom. Children love this simple pudding, especially when it's served with fresh or tinned fruit.

Heat 1½ cups (375 mL) of the milk in top of a double boiler over medium heat. Mix cornstarch, salt and sugar together in a small bowl and combine with remaining ½ cup (125 mL) of milk. Add cornstarch mixture to hot milk and cook, stirring constantly until thickened. Continue cooking on low heat for a further 15 minutes, stirring occasionally. Add part of mixture to slightly beaten egg yolks. Combine and add egg mixture to double boiler. Cook for 2 minutes. Remove from heat and stir in butter and vanilla. Pour into serving dishes and allow to cool before serving.

To prevent the pudding from forming a skin as it cools, make a parchment circle to fit each dish. The hole in the middle allows steam to vent.

2 cups	milk	500 mL
2 Tbsp.	cornstarch	25 mL
¼ tsp.	salt	1 mL
¼ cup	sugar	50 mL
2	egg yolks, slightly beaten	2
2 tsp.	butter	10 mL
1 tsp.	vanilla	5 mL

SERVES 4

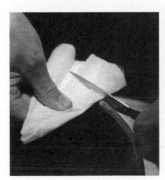

Fresh Peaches
and Raspberry Purée

❦

6	peaches	6
1½ cups	sugar	375 mL
2 cups	water	500 mL
1 cup	raspberries	250 mL
1 cup	water	250 mL
1 Tbsp.	icing sugar	15 mL
1 Tbsp.	cornstarch	15 mL
	vanilla ice cream	

SERVES 6

This is a childhood favourite called Peach Melba. We didn't always have the luxury of using fresh peaches, so very often it was made quickly using canned peaches. The raspberry purée can be used as a topping for cheesecake or just plain ice cream.

Score the peaches with a paring knife. Place in boiling water for 15 to 30 seconds, then plunge them into ice-cold water. Using a paring knife, remove the skin from the peaches. Run a knife down the seam of the peach until you hit the stone. Turn the knife to remove the stone.

Place the sugar and the 2 cups water in a pot and bring to a simmer. Place the halved peaches in the hot syrup and poach for 5 minutes until tender.

In a small saucepan put fresh raspberries, 1 cup water, icing sugar and cornstarch. Mix together over medium heat, stirring constantly for 5 minutes, being careful not to let the mixture burn. Remove from heat and let cool slightly. Pass through a fine sieve. Set aside and allow to cool.

To serve, place 2 peach halves in a dessert bowl, followed by a scoop of vanilla ice cream. Top the ice cream with raspberry purée.

Maple Syrup Ice Cream

This recipe calls for a cooked custard preparation. There are a couple of advantages to this. You end up with a very creamy, smooth, rich texture, and the flavours have a chance to infuse. Try to make up the custard the day before so it will be chilled properly. The leftover egg whites can be frozen or used to make baked meringues to serve the ice cream in.

¾ cup	maple syrup	175 mL
4	egg yolks	4
2 cups	light cream	500 mL
2 cups	whipping cream	500 mL

YIELDS 4 CUPS (1 L)

Place maple syrup in a heavy pot and simmer until it is reduced by about half. Remove from heat and cool to room temperature. In a stainless steel bowl, combine the maple syrup and the egg yolks and whisk until well blended.

In a heavy-bottomed stainless steel pot, heat the light cream. When just below a simmer, add a small amount of it to the yolk mixture, thus tempering it. Pour tempered mixture into pot and cook until the custard coats the back of a spoon. Remove from heat and stir in heavy whipping cream. Let cool completely. It can be refrigerated overnight. Freeze in ice cream maker.

Toasted Coconut Cheesecake with Mango Purée

If you can't picture yourself under a palm tree watching a neon-coloured sunset as a turquoise ocean laps at the white sand at your feet, just take a bite of this creamy tropical cheesecake.

CRUST		
1¼ cups	graham wafer crumbs	300 mL
2 Tbsp.	sugar	30 mL
3 Tbsp.	butter, melted	45 mL

FILLING		
½ cup	unsweetened shredded coconut	125 mL
1 lb.	cream cheese	500 g
¾ cup	sour cream	175 mL
¾ cup	sugar	175 mL
4	eggs, slightly beaten	4
1 tsp.	vanilla	5 mL
¼ cup	coconut milk	50 mL

CRUST: Preheat oven to 300°F (150°C).

In a 10-inch (25 cm) springform pan, mix together graham wafer crumbs, sugar and butter. Pat firmly into pan and up sides. (If you line the bottom of the pan with parchment paper, it will be very easy to slide the cheesecake from the pan for serving and storage.)

Bake for 5 minutes.

FILLING: Place coconut on a baking sheet and toast in 300°F (150°C) oven for 5 minutes or until golden. Keep and eye on it so it doesn't burn. Remove from oven and set aside.

Mix together the cream cheese and sour cream until smooth. Blend in sugar and slightly beaten eggs. Add vanilla, coconut milk and toasted coconut. Blend well. Pour on top of partially baked graham crust and bake at 300°F (150°C) for 1 hour. Remove from oven and allow to cool for 10 minutes before adding the topping.

MANGO PURÉE: While cheesecake is baking, place mango chunks in a saucepan along with the sugar, water and lime juice. Cook uncovered on medium-high heat for 15 to 20 minutes until cooked. Set aside to cool. Put in a blender or food processor and process until completely smooth. Refrigerate and chill until needed.

This mango purée can be frozen for later use. It is also delicious as a topping for ice cream.

TOPPING: Whisk together the sour cream, coconut milk, sugar and vanilla until smooth. Spread on top of the cheesecake with a spatula. Bake in 300°F (150°C) oven for 5 minutes. Serve small wedges with lots of mango purée napped over.

	MANGO PURÉE	
4 cups	peeled and cut up mango (2-3 mangoes)	1 L
⅓ cup	sugar	75 mL
2 cups	water	500 mL
1 Tbsp.	lime juice	15 mL

	TOPPING	
1½ cups	sour cream	375 mL
1 Tbsp.	coconut milk	15 mL
¼ cup	sugar	50 mL
¼ tsp.	vanilla	1 mL

SERVES 8

Peanut Butter and Chocolate Chunk Cookies

½ cup	unsalted butter, soft	125 mL
½ cup	natural peanut butter	125 mL
½ cup	white sugar	125 mL
¾ cup	brown sugar	175 mL
1	egg	1
½ cup	oatmeal	125 mL
1 cup	flour	250 mL
½ tsp.	baking powder	2 mL
¾ tsp.	baking soda	4 mL
¼ tsp.	salt	1 mL
5 oz.	milk chocolate, cut in ½-inch (1 cm) chunks	150 g

YIELDS 2½ DOZEN

It's the classic case of the missing cookies—as soon as these are baked they disappear from the counter. The only visible evidence seems to be smiling faces.

The finely ground oatmeal adds a nice texture.

Preheat oven to 375°F (190°).

In a mixing bowl, cream butter and peanut butter together. Add white sugar and brown sugar and blend well. Add egg and beat until fluffy.

Grind oatmeal fine in a food processor. Combine all dry ingredients in a bowl. Add to the batter and mix until blended. Stir in chocolate chunks. Cover and chill for 1 hour.

Roll spoonfuls of dough into 1-inch (2.5 cm) balls and place on a lightly greased baking sheet. Flatten with a fork dipped in flour, forming a crisscross pattern on top. Bake for 10 minutes, until golden but still a bit soft. Let cool for a few minutes on baking sheet, then remove with a metal spatula and let cool completely on a wire rack.

Building Blocks

Béchamel Sauce

2 Tbsp.	butter	30 mL
2 Tbsp.	unbleached flour	30 mL
2 cups	milk	500 mL
	salt and pepper	

YIELDS 2 CUPS (500 ML)

This basic white sauce is a foundation of many wonderful variations. Add herbs, capers, white wine or sweated onions, and you have something to improve any dish.

Melt butter in heavy saucepan. Add the flour and cook gently, stirring constantly until the flour is well incorporated. You will know it is ready when it leaves the sides of the pan and changes to a slightly lighter colour.

Remove the butter and flour mixture from heat and pour in the milk. Return pan to medium heat and bring the béchamel to a boil, stirring constantly for 5 minutes. Season to taste with salt and pepper. Use at once or cool, cover and refrigerate.

Quick Tomato Sauce

❦

This sauce can be made ahead and kept refrigerated for 5 days. I make it every week because it's so handy to have around. You'll find it called for in many of the recipes throughout the book.

The secret is to keep the lid on while it's simmering. It results in a bright red, intensely flavoured sauce.

Heat the olive oil and butter in a large pot. Stir in the chopped onions and garlic and sweat them over medium heat with the lid on. When the onions are tender, add the chopped canned tomatoes. (A hand blender works well for chopping.) Add sugar and salt and pepper to taste. Simmer covered for ½ hour. If you will be using it in a recipe that calls for further cooking, reduce simmering time to 15 minutes.

VARIATION: *Cream of Tomato Soup*

Add 1 cup (250 mL) vegetable or chicken stock when you add the tomatoes. Simmer covered on medium heat for 45 minutes. Let cool to room temperature. Pour into blender and purée until smooth. Pass soup through a strainer to remove seeds. Pour soup back into pot and add 1 cup (250 mL) cream. Whisk and bring to a simmer. Do not boil. Season with salt and pepper. Serve with Big Dippers (page 116).

1 Tbsp.	olive oil	15 mL
1 Tbsp.	butter	15 mL
1	onion, chopped	1
1	clove garlic, minced	1
28-oz. tin	whole plum tomatoes, chopped	796 mL
1 tsp.	sugar	5 mL
	salt and pepper	

YIELDS 3 CUPS (796 ML)

August Pasta Sauce

❦

2 Tbsp.	olive oil	30 mL
½ cup	finely chopped onion	125 mL
½ cup	chopped red peppers	125 mL
½ cup	chopped yellow peppers	125 mL
½ cup	chopped eggplant	125 mL
2	cloves garlic, chopped	2
3-4	large ripe tomatoes, blanched, skinned and chopped	3-4 large
¼ cup	chopped black olives, pitted	50 mL
¼ cup	sundried tomatoes in oil	50 mL
1 cup	water or tomato juice	250 mL
1 Tbsp.	chopped fresh basil or oregano	15 mL
	salt and pepper	
¾ lb.	dried pasta (enough for 4-6 people)	350 g
½-1 cup	freshly grated Parmesan cheese	125-250 mL
4-6	leaves basil, chopped	4-6

SERVES 4 TO 6

August is the time of year when all of these ingredients are in their prime. The flavours reflect a wonderful natural sweetness. This sauce freezes well. It's like revisiting summer to have it on a miserable day.

Combine it with your favourite pasta. We like to use a spaghetti or fettuccini.

Place large soup pot on medium heat and pour in oil. Add the onions, peppers, eggplant and garlic. Cover and cook until the vegetables are partially cooked and the onions are transparent. Add the chopped tomatoes, olives, sundried tomatoes and tomato juice. Add fresh basil and season lightly with salt and pepper. Continue to cook uncovered on low heat for a further 20 minutes.

While sauce is cooking prepare pasta following directions on package.

Toss the sauce with freshly cooked pasta and grated Parmesan cheese. Scatter with fresh chopped basil and serve in warm pasta bowls.

Bread Sauce

When I was a kid in Wales we always had bread sauce served with a whole roast chicken or turkey. It went right along with the stuffing and the meat. I think that this sauce, with its subtle warmth of cloves, would be considered haute cuisine if it had originated any-where but the British Isles.

Break off the little seeds from the top of the cloves and discard, other-wise they will flavour the dish too much. Spike the onion with the cloves.

Combine all of the ingredients in a small saucepan. Place on medium-low heat and bring just to a simmer. Cook for approximately 20 to 30 minutes on low heat, stirring gently with a wooden spoon making sure the sauce doesn't stick or burn on the bottom.

Remove the onion before serving. The sauce will still have a bit of texture when it's done. If it is too thick simply add a bit more milk.

6	whole cloves	6
½	small onion	½
1 cup	milk	250 mL
	pinch salt	
1 cup	cubed white bread, crust removed	250 mL

SERVES 4

Orange Honey Dressing

This is great as a light citrus summer dressing for grilled fish or crunchy salad greens.

Combine all of the ingredients in a screw-top jar. Place on the lid and shake really well. Refrigerate until required.

⅓ cup	freshly squeezed orange juice (1 orange)	7 mL
1 tsp.	liquid honey	5 mL
⅓ cup	olive or canola oil	75 mL
	small pinch salt	
	small pinch or twist of pepper	

YIELDS ⅔ CUP (150 ML)

Fresh Basil Sorbet

2	stems fresh basil (¼ cup/50 mL chopped leaves)	2
1¼ cups	peeled and chopped green apples (2 apples)	300 mL
½ cup	peeled and chopped pear (1 pear)	125 mL
3 Tbsp.	lemon juice	45 mL
⅓ cup	sugar	75 mL
3 cups	water	750 mL

YIELDS 6 CUPS (1.5 L)

Sorbets are great at dinner parties. They give me a bit more time between courses to finish off the main course preparation. For an elegant presentation, place a single scoop in a champagne cup or martini glass.

Pull off the basil leaves off stems. Set leaves aside and reserve stems.

Place the apple, pear, 2 basil stems, lemon juice, sugar and water in a pot. Bring the ingredients to a boil. Turn down and let simmer on low heat until the fruit is very tender.

Remove from heat and let the mixture cool completely. Remove the basil stems and discard. Purée the mixture in a food processor or food mill.

Chop the basil leaves into fine strips and add to the sorbet mixture.

Freeze the sorbet in an ice cream maker following the manufacturer's directions. You can also make a granita without an ice cream maker. Put the liquid in a baking pan in the freezer and stir it with a fork every hour or so until it's frozen. This will have a grainier texture than the sorbet.

Roasted Roma Tomatoes

❧

These roasted tomatoes are irresistible. They're delicious hot, right out of the oven alongside a roast. They can also be served cold, tossed in with a salad or as part of an antipasto tray. A couple of these will also add a rich tomato flavour to a sauce.

Roma tomatoes—even those waxy underripe ones that you get at the supermarket year round—are the best variety for roasting because they generally contain less moisture.

8	large Roma tomatoes	8
½ tsp.	salt	2 mL
¼ cup	extra virgin olive oil	50 mL

SERVES 4

Preheat oven to 350°F (180°C).

Wash and dry the tomatoes. Cut them in half lengthwise and place in a large bowl. Season with salt and toss with oil. Line a cookie sheet with parchment paper. Place tomato halves cut side up on paper (otherwise you end up with too much moisture on the sheet). Roast on top rack of oven for approximately 1 hour or until caramelized. They can be served straight out of the oven or allowed to cool.

Tobiko Cream

❧

1 cup	whipping cream	250 mL
1 Tbsp.	tobiko roe	15 mL

SERVES 6

Tobiko, or flying fish roe, has a rich orange colour and a crunchy texture. It's readily available at any Japanese food store, usually in the frozen fish section. I love to use this cream as a garnish for seafood soups. You could also combine the tobiko roe with soft cream cheese and use it as a spread for seafood wraps.

Whip the cream until fairly thick, then fold in the tobiko roe. Refrigerate until needed.

Yogurt Horseradish Dip

❧

1 cup	plain yogurt	250 mL
1 cup	mayonnaise	250 mL
1 Tbsp.	creamed horseradish	15 mL
	juice of half a lemon	
2 Tbsp.	chopped fresh dill	30 mL
	freshly ground pepper to taste	

YIELDS 2 CUPS (500 ML)

This is a great foil for crunchy raw vegetables such as radishes, carrots, celery, broccoli, cauliflower, cucumber and tomato. If you like it hotter, increase the horseradish.

Blend the yogurt and mayonnaise well. Add remaining ingredients.

Crunchy Pub Onions

These pale pink onion rounds remind me of the pickled onions Mum used to make when I was a kid. They're also found in every pub throughout the British Isles as a staple in the ploughman's lunch. They're great with grilled chops, steak or hard cheeses.

I usually make these up as gifts for friends and customers and pack them into empty Dijon mustard jars (the type with the rubber seal and metal clamp). Any wide-mouthed jar will do.

This recipe can be doubled.

4	red onions	4
	boiling water	
2 Tbsp.	liquid honey	25 mL
1 tsp.	peppercorns	5 mL
½ cup	cold water	125 mL
1½ cups	white vinegar	375 mL

YIELDS 4 CUPS (1 L)

Peel onions and cut crosswise into ¼-inch (5 mm) thick slices. Do not separate into rings. Discard the root at the end. Place in a bowl, being careful to keep the slices together. Cover with boiling water and allow to stand for 5 minutes. Drain off hot water.

Wash, rinse and sterilize a wide-mouthed 4 cup (1 L) jar. Pour in the honey and whole peppercorns. Start to pack the onion slices into the jar, making sure to keep the onions in slices. When the jar is full, pour in the cold water and then the white vinegar. Screw on lid. Keep in refrigerator for 5 days until onions are completely pickled. Once opened, they will keep in your fridge for 3 to 4 weeks.

My Nana's Piccalilli

4 lbs.	vegetables: cauliflower, marrow or zucchini, green tomato, runner beans, and shallots or onions	2 kg
2 Tbsp	salt	25 mL
4 cups	malt or red wine vinegar	1 L
2 Tbsp.	mixed whole spice or pickling spice	25 mL
2 Tbsp.	turmeric	25 mL
1 Tbsp.	ground ginger	15 mL
2 Tbsp.	dry mustard	25 mL
2 Tbsp.	cornstarch	25 mL
2 Tbsp.	vinegar	25 mL
2¼ cups	sugar	550 mL

YIELDS 12 CUPS (3 L)

If anything takes me back home, it's this pickle—a real British classic. Each of these vegetables adds a different texture and taste to the piccalilli. Everybody has his or her own favourite. I would always try and find the whole shallot. Other people might like the cauliflower or the beans.

This is a great way to use up green tomatoes, which are essential to the recipe.

Roughly chop the vegetables. Slice the runner beans. If the shallots are small they are nice left whole. Place vegetables in a bowl, toss with salt and leave in the refrigerator overnight. The salt will draw out moisture. This moisture needs to be drained off through a colander.

Put the whole spice in a muslin bag and boil gently in the vinegar for about an hour. Remove spice and add vegetables (do not rinse). Cook until soft. Mix turmeric, ginger, mustard and cornstarch together in 2 Tbsp. (25ml) vinegar, and add to the pot. Last, add sugar. Boil and stir until mixture is fairly thick.

Put into sterilized jars and seal. This piccalilli can be used anytime with savoury dishes, and keeps for years if processed.

Berry Vinegar

❧

Making vinegars from fresh berries is something we do every summer at the restaurant. The same recipe works for any fresh berry, but I especially love raspberry vinegar.

2 cups	white wine vinegar	500 mL
1 cup	berries, cleaned	250 mL

YIELDS 2 CUPS (500 ML)

Pour vinegar into a jar that will hold 3 cups (750 mL). Mash berries (not necessary for raspberries) and add to vinegar. Allow to sit in a cool dark place for 4 weeks. Strain and refrigerate.

This will keep in a cool place for up to 3 months. After that the vinegar loses its freshness.

VARIATION: *Chive Flower Vinegar*

When the chive flowers bloom, give them a couple of days for the bees to get at them, then harvest, wash and allow to dry. Using the same proportions as above, add chive flowers to vinegar and allow to sit for 4 weeks. Strain and refrigerate.

Balsamic Essence

1 cup	balsamic vinegar	250 mL

YIELDS ⅓ CUP (75 ML)

I started making a list of all the things that could benefit from the fruity, tangy high notes this glaze provides, and it just kept getting longer and longer: fish, poultry, steak, pork loin, grilled vegetables, roasted vegetables, roasted pears . . .

This is also really effective squeezed in an abstract pattern next to the food, and maybe crisscrossed with some infused oil.

Pour vinegar into wide pan over medium-high heat. Simmer uncovered until reduced by ⅔. Cool and store in plastic squeeze bottle.

VARIATION: Do the same thing with equal parts balsamic and raspberry vinegar.

Basil or Parsley Oil

Infused oils have become a restaurant staple. By simply spotting a few drops here and there around a finished dish. you can add intense flavour bursts and dramatic colour.

They can be brushed over vegetables, poultry or seafood prior to grilling. They also make a great swirl on top of soups and stews. If you keep them in plastic squeeze bottles you can apply just the amount you want, just where you want.

Wash and dry the herbs. Chop roughly. Place in a food processor with the extra virgin olive oil. Pulse the mixture for 1 minute. Pour the oil mixture into a sterilized container and let sit for 24 hours in the refrigerator.

Line a fine sieve with cheesecloth. Strain the oil through the sieve, pressing when necessary.

Basil oil will be a greenish-gold. Parsley oil will be brilliant green.

Keep refrigerated in a clean container. The oil will keep for up to 2 weeks.

¾ cup	basil leaves, packed or	175 mL
1 cup	parsley leaves, packed	250 mL
2 cups	extra virgin olive oil	500 mL

YIELDS 2 CUPS (500 ML)

Chicken Stock

1¼ lbs.	chicken bones or 1 whole chicken carcass	625 g
1	medium onion, chopped	1
1	medium carrot, chopped	1
1	stalk celery, chopped	1
2	sprigs fresh thyme	2
1	whole bay leaf	1
1	sprig fresh parsley	1
1 tsp.	whole peppercorns	5 mL
8 cups	cold water	2 L

YIELDS 4 CUPS (1 L)

We've started giving cooking classes at the restaurant, and I have to admit, I've been astonished at the number of people who don't make stocks as a matter of course—or don't even know how. So I'll keep saying it: nothing will improve your cooking more than homemade stocks. Save your meat and chicken trimmings in the freezer until you have enough.

This recipe can easily be doubled in volume.

Place all ingredients in a large stockpot. Cover with the cold water and place on medium-high heat. When the stock has reached boiling point, turn the temperature down to low and simmer for 2 hours, skimming off any foam. Strain, cool and refrigerate or freeze until needed.

Crab Stock

Place all of the ingredients in a large stockpot. Cover with the cold water. Place pot on medium-high heat. Bring to a boil, turn down heat to low and simmer for 1½ to 2 hours.

Stock should have reduced down to ⅓ to ½ of its original volume. Strain and cool if not required immediately. Can be frozen for up to 2 months.

2	cooked crab shells	2
1	stalk celery, chopped	1
2	carrots, chopped	2
1	onion, chopped	1
2	cloves garlic, chopped	2
2	leaves basil, chopped	2
1	sprig parsley, chopped	1
2	ripe tomatoes, chopped	2
8 cups	cold water	2 l

YIELDS 4 CUPS (1 L)

Lamb Stock

Place bone, trimmings, chopped vegetables and herbs in a roasting pan. Drizzle with vegetable oil and place in a 375°F (190°C) oven. Roast for 45 minutes, stirring occasionally to make sure the bones and vegetables are browning evenly.

Remove from oven, and place bone and trimmings in stockpot. Pour the water into the baking dish. Stir around to pick up all the roasting juices from the pan. Now pour the water and juices over the bones. On medium-high heat bring to a boil. Turn down heat and skim off any foam. Simmer for approximately 1 hour. Strain and freeze. This is an excellent base from which to create meat sauces.

1	lamb leg bone and trimmings	1
1	onion, chopped	1
2	carrots, chopped	2
1	stalk celery, chopped	1
1	bay leaf	1
1 tsp.	rosemary leaves, optional	5 mL
1 tsp.	salt	5 mL
½ tsp.	whole peppercorns	2 mL
2 Tbsp.	vegetable oil	30 mL
8 cups	cold water	2 L

YIELDS 6 CUPS (1.5 L)

Index